Teachers and Learners

The Interactive Process of Education

Teachers and Learners

The Interactive Process of Education

ALFRED H. GORMAN

Professor of Education
Montclair State College
New Jersey

Allyn and Bacon, Inc.   Boston

Preface

This is a book for teachers who wish to improve that area of teaching that lies within the sphere of interactive behavior in the classroom. The basic assumption underlying the material to follow is that teaching and learning is a process of communication among individuals in a group setting. If such an assumption is a valid one, it follows as a first step that a professional teacher should be aware of theory and practice in human communication. As a second step he must then seek to internalize the material into his behavioral repertoire.

To accomplish such internalization, whether the book is used in a college classroom, in an inservice education program, or by an individual teacher, it is suggested that the material be treated in four successive stages. First, the book should be read carefully and discussed. Second, the class (including its teacher) should try out some of the exercises including reactions to them. Third, the materials should be reviewed to check as to whether understanding of them has been deepened by the exercises. Fourth, class members should attempt, perhaps after further reading in the field, to produce approaches and exercises adapted to their own personal needs. Where it is possible, a fifth step would include trying out some of these approaches in a practice-teaching situation.

Thus the teacher—or prospective teacher—dealing personally with interactive experiences should begin to develop skills both for communicating his knowledge of subject matter and for setting the classroom stage for student learning. In turn, this stage setting should create a readiness for teaching and learning by reducing the social distance between teacher and student while maintaining mutual respect.

Such a notion is certainly not a new or even an unusual one. Great teachers have always been able to cut through barriers to communication and reach their students. In addition, they have been personally flexible enough to allow their students to reach them.

One central value in all good teaching is that of student growth toward greater maturity and self-direction. This growth can be enhanced or inhibited to a marked degree by teacher behavior in and out of the classroom. When inhibition results, the teacher has not touched the student and the student has not really touched—or been touched by—the subject matter.

Teachers throughout recorded history have tried in various ways to reach their students, yet problems of passive learners and dominating teachers still exist. In the American society, which attempts education for *all* its youth, these problems have become more and more acute. The culturally deprived child, the growth of a delinquent subculture, the increasing numbers of dropouts, the racial minorities who seek integration into the larger society, the underachieving college-bound—all these youngsters present the school with an acute challenge that cannot be ignored or relegated to textbook theorizing. It is for the teacher who recognizes these problems and who seeks specific answers to the question, "What can I do to reach my students?" that this book has been written. Its objective is the clarification in behavioral terms of just what does happen when students and teachers interact and how this happening can be examined, evaluated, and improved.

Materials are organized under three main headings: (1) the past, present, and future of teaching and learning behavior; (2) a conceptual framework for the teaching act; and (3) methods of approaching, developing, elaborating, evaluating, and improving classroom communication on both intellectual and emotional levels. Since the subject under discussion is interactive behavior, such important aspects of teacher education as philosophy, psychology of the learner, daily and unit lesson planning, curriculum construction, textbook selection, test construction, reporting of pupil progress, and the like are *not* dealt with here. It is assumed that they will receive their proper amount of attention elsewhere.

All the approaches detailed in the following chapters have been tested by the author in group learning situations. While they by no means constitute a bag of tricks that will work for anyone in any situation, they have proved useful in opening many new avenues of communication for teachers and students.

Effective teaching is always a difficult and demanding enterprise. If it were an easy one, there would be far fewer poor teachers and frustrated students. More often than not, however, "poor teaching" is really the existence of an interaction problem that is allowed to go unresolved. The material in this book does not do away with problems, but it does suggest ways in which they can be faced, defined, and solved. The reader who wishes to master this material can expect hard work, an intellectual and emotional challenge, and some frustrations and failures along the way. But if he is able to internalize and use the theory and methodology, he can also expect the greatest reward of teaching—the feeling that he has helped others to personal growth.

A.H.G.

Contents

1 TEACHING AND LEARNING: PAST, PRESENT, AND FUTURE   1

THE CHANGING SCHOOL   2
CURRENT ALTERNATIVES TO CURRENT PRACTICES   4
TEACHING AND LEARNING   7
SUMMARIZATION WITH NO FEEDBACK   20

2 THE TEACHER AND THE CLASS: A THEORETICAL FRAMEWORK FOR INTERACTION   22

THE THEORY   22
THE FRAMEWORK   31
STRUCTURE, PROCESS, AND ATTITUDE IN THE CLASSROOM   34
AIMS OF IMPROVED CLASSROOM INTERACTION   40
PUTTING THE THEORY TO WORK   41

3 CLASSROOM INTERACTION PROCESSES   42

INTERNAL GROUP VARIABLES   42
ULTIMATE GOALS   53
SPECIFIC OBJECTIVES   54
PROCESS IN TEACHING AND LEARNING   55
CONTENT AND PROCESS BEHAVIORS   57
PROCESS AND THE TOTAL GROUP   62

4 INTERACTION EXERCISES   63

ROLE PLAYING   63
BUILDING THE GROUP   81
LISTENING SKILL SESSION   88
NON-DIRECTIVE DISCUSSION LEADERSHIP   90
AGREE-DISAGREE EXERCISE   98

Buzz Groups 102
Three-Step Design 104
Case Analysis 109
In General 119

5 REACTION AND EVALUATION INSTRUMENTS 120

Subject Matter and the Process of Education 121
Purposes of Process Evaluation 123
Data Gathering Instruments 123
Observation of Others 139
Personal Reaction to Class Sessions 146
Ratings of Others 155
Evaluation and Reaction in General 163

6 PROCESS COMMUNICATION AND THE ROLE OF THE SCHOOL 165

Traditional Treatment of School Problems 165
Process in Teaching 170

BIBLIOGRAPHY 183

1

Teaching
and
Learning:
Past Present and Future

EARLY IN THE existence of human life on our planet men and women began to cluster in groups. In the give and take of living together, they rapidly formed customs, rituals, communication systems, social institutions, values, and tools for the mastery, or partial mastery, of their physical environment. Since even the most primitive cultures had to be passed on from the elders to the young if the society were to be maintained, some form of schooling was needed, and efficiency soon demanded that instruction be given to groups of learners rather than handled on a one-to-one basis. Traditionally, then, throughout the history of man, teaching and learning has taken place in a group setting.

With the onward march of civilization and the development of more and more complex societies, increasing individual specialization became the norm. For similar reasons, the schooling of a higher and higher percentage of the total population became a necessity. To meet these needs, school systems have grown rapidly, but never quite rapidly enough. Each succeeding generation adds to the problems and anxieties of educators who can rarely take time from their daily tasks to stand back and analyze what they are doing.

Given such mounting pressures, it seems a wonder that the schools have accomplished as much as they have. Even in American life, where mass education has long been an accepted value, problems have multiplied rapidly in the twentieth century as the dream of schooling for all has become more of a reality with each passing decade. School districts all over the land find themselves in a constant race to provide physical plants and teaching staff for the hordes of students. Not only must schools deal with an increasing percentage of a population explosion, but they must deal with it over a longer time span. Even the notion of twelve years of schooling for all is being increased at one end by the nursery school and at the other by the junior college.

THE CHANGING SCHOOL

A more subtle challenge than need for buildings and staff is presented by the percentage increases. Today, large numbers of youngsters whose aspirations do not include college entrance are being pressured to stay longer in the schools. This factor has meant—in the literature if not in practice—the modification of the high school, primarily a college-preparing institution, to meet a wider span of student needs. And as if all this were not enough for an institution that has never had the time or money to really study itself, the school has been ordered to take on additional tasks. In the face of what is seen by some observers as the breakdown of neighborhood, church, and family influence, teachers are being expected to enculturate students and develop their moral and spiritual values. In addition, societal problems in terms of culturally deprived students, racial integration, juvenile delinquency, school dropouts, mental health, and human relationships are currently being added to the previous tasks of passing on the cultural heritage, developing citizenship, and increasing skills in the 3 R's.[1]

[1] In recent years a number of books and motion pictures have dealt with pressing student needs in the areas of love, respect, and dignity as a prerequisite to learning subject matter. The fact that they have received sympathetic attention from so many readers and viewers seems to indicate a growing awareness of the importance of affect in the classroom. The reader should take special note

These demands and others of a similar nature are being made by a society long identified with rapid change. With simpler occupations being constantly automated out of existence, with the reality of a cold and a warm war plus the threat of a hot nuclear destruction, with the stresses of a permissively brought up generation rampant on a field of traditional teacher authoritarianism, with the pressures of constant test-taking and test-passing to stay in the mainstream of required schooling, young people are responding with deviant behavior. A recent cause for concern in this area is the increasing number of suicides at elementary as well as secondary school levels. But the reported statistics of hippies, dropouts, and suicides have not as yet reached a critical phase. What is really more alarming is the unexplored problem of the psychological dropout, where the body keeps coming to school though the mind has left long ago.

Into this violent and ever shifting maze of needs and problems thousands of young teachers march bravely each fall armed with a fair overview of a fairly narrow teaching field, a disconnected smattering of psychology and philosophy to which a dash of sociology may have been added, an almost morbid fear of being "too idealistic," and varying shades of apprehension concerning reactionary administrators and student behavior problems.

In too many cases, they march into egg-crate shaped schools where in similar sized rooms single teachers face student aggregates[2] of twenty-five to forty or more. Activities of

---

of books such as Kaufman, Bel, *Up the Down Staircase*, Englewood Cliffs, N.J.: Prentice-Hall, 1964; Kohl, Herbert, *36 Children*, New York: The New American Library, 1967; and Kozol, Jonathan, *Death at an Early Age*, Boston: Houghton-Mifflin, 1967. Pertinent films include *Up the Down Staircase*, *To Sir With Love*, and *The Blackboard Jungle*.

[2]The term *aggregate* as used here indicates a collection of human beings brought together to accomplish some task. An *aggregate* differs from a *group* in that members of an *aggregate* maintain their individual defenses at all times, interact in a formal manner, refuse to deal with their feelings about each other, and remain fairly tentative, untrusting, and suspicious of each other. The typical school classroom is a setting in which students do not know other students, and no one really knows the teacher as a person. The *aggregate* as a classroom situation is seen in Figure 4 while the class as a *group* appears in Figure 5.

the day include primarily one-way communication in periods of forty to fifty minutes at a time. Regardless of the state of student readiness at the end of each hour of instruction, a loud bell signals frenzied activity throughout the school as classroom contents are emptied into the halls and reassembled as different aggregates so that they may start the process all over again. It is doubtless a factor of their closeness to the situation and the state of conformity imposed upon teachers and students alike that the comical side of this rigid structure rarely becomes an issue in the profession or in the student government. It is only recently—and then very tentatively—that there has been a re-surgence of the Progressive questions raised by John Dewey and the later advocates of the core curriculum.[3] Most teachers seem to accept the assumption that students can carry on most learning experiences in groups of thirty, and that they can turn motivation on and off in Pavlovian fashion at the bidding of the passing bell. Yet new ideas *do* exist, and some are beginning to be used.

CURRENT ALTERNATIVES TO TRADITIONAL PRACTICES

During the past several years, alternatives in terms of structure have been developed in response to the needs for flexibility in staff utilization and instructional procedures.

The Trump Plan

The proposals by Lloyd Trump[4] suggest that purposes of teaching differentiate the structure to be used according to the intent of the teacher and his approach to the subject. Accordingly, for initial presentation of a concept, an overview of a unit, a visiting panel of experts, or for some similar purpose, a student group of 250 to 500 students would be as sensible as

[3]For a good historical look at the rise of the Progressive Movement in American schools, see Cremin, Lawrence A., *The Transformation of the School*, New York: Knopf, 1961. For a basic work dealing with the concept of the core curriculum, see Alberty, Harold B., *Reorganizing the High School Curriculum*, New York: Macmillan, 1962.

[4]These proposals are set forth in Trump, J. Lloyd and Dorsey Baynham, *Focus on Change*, Chicago: Rand McNally, 1961.

30, and valuable teacher time could be saved for other instructional or planning activities. On the other hand, for intense seminar-type discussion, a student group of 12 to 14 members is a maximum size. Such work cannot be done effectively in the traditional 30 student group. Finally, for development of self-direction and of methods of inquiry that will remain after schooling ends, each pupil should have the experience of working individually in some areas of learning. Accordingly, the Trump Plan calls for an end to across-the-board scheduling of the one-period-a-day type and suggests Large Group (100 or more), Small Group (14 or less), and Individual (1 or 2 students) experiences within the framework of the high-school program.

The Non-Graded School

Another challenge to the historical lockstep structure lies in the concept of the non-graded school.[5] Here, students are scheduled individually, make continual progress at their individual rates of learning, and complete the secondary school program when *they* are ready. For a long unimaginative time, educators have kept the time of instruction constant (year-long courses and a four-year experience for all) and varied the learning (A-B-C-D-F). Recent experimentation with teaching machines and programed learning suggests that it is feasible to reverse this procedure.[6] Thus the time of instruction may vary (seven months of a year for one student, nine for another, eleven for another) while the learning becomes constant (all students get A, with brighter people getting a chance to study more subjects). In the non-graded school, the foolishness of repeating an entire year of a subject would disappear. Students

[5]Two valuable sources of information on non-graded programs are Goodlad, John I., and Robert H. Anderson, *The Non-Graded Elementary School*, New York: Harcourt Brace, 1959, and Brown, Bartley Frank, *The Non-Graded High School*, Englewood Cliffs, N.J.: Prentice-Hall, 1963.

[6]New programed materials are being developed each year in a wide variety of subject areas. Helpful books in this field include: Deterline, William A., *Programed Instruction*, Englewood Cliffs, N.J.: Prentice-Hall, 1962; Lysaught, Jerome P., and Clarence M. Williams, *A Guide to Programmed Instruction*, New York: Wiley, 1963; and Mager, Robert F., *Preparing Objectives for Programmed Instruction*, San Francisco: Fearon Publishers, 1962.

would make continuous progress without skipping anything or failing anything. More able students would either leave earlier for college or go more deeply into the disciplines for which they showed unusual aptitude.

Team Teaching

In concert with the Trump Plan and the Non-Graded School, the practice of team teaching is beginning to interest teachers and administrators throughout the country.[7] The Trump organization calls for a team leader, staff teachers, teaching assistants from undergraduate programs, and clerical help. Other plans vary from two teachers who correlate their teaching of separate courses to staff groups representing several subject areas who attempt to develop a cohesive whole out of the traditional separate subject approach. Done well, team teaching can bring specific teacher strengths to larger numbers of students. In this notion of joint planning, teaching, and evaluating lies one of the first ideas for making education a real professional endeavor to come along in a generation.

Further Innovations

Innovations are currently the order of the day in the schools. Libraries, audio-visual programs, community resources, paperback books, and the mimeograph machine have merged in the sparkling new field of instructional materials. Programed materials are giving new flexibility to learners, while devices such as the overhead projector extend the teacher's versatility. Highly sophisticated tape-recording facilities have revolution-ized many foreign language programs, and more imaginative uses of educational television are being developed each year.

Teachers have passed through the initial stages of the "new math," fresh programs have been developed in the physi-cal sciences, the structural linguists are beginning to affect the teaching of English, and history teachers are now attempting to teach the methods of inquiry of their discipline, replacing

[7]For a good basic picture of this innovation see Shaplin, Judson T., and Henry F. Olds, Jr., eds. *Team Teaching*, New York: Harper, 1964.

the traditional fact-cramming approach. The social studies are really becoming social studies with the development of courses in sociology, anthropology, and psychology at the high-school level. Business education is moving from a simple typing and shorthand image into a complex treatment of the modern business office complete with computers. Industrial arts has gone beyond the production of pump lamps into a preparation for general industrial processes. Home economics is shedding its cooking and sewing aura in favor of a human relations approach to family living in a modern society. Physical educators have stopped blowing whistles and throwing balls up into the air to develop effective programs in general physical fitness and lifetime participation sports. Areas of art and music are being merged with history courses to combat general artistic illiteracy, special approaches are being mounted in speech arts and therapy, and programs of sex education have already begun in many schools.

Work-study programs are growing in numbers and effectiveness, and even the egg-crate school has been challenged by modern educator-architects. The structure of the schools themselves is in flux, with the junior high school in the 6-3-3 framework giving way to a middle school in a 4-4-4 organization. All these activities are beginning very slowly but steadily to change the face of American education, and teacher education is moving with its usual turtle speed to catch up and stay abreast.

TEACHING AND LEARNING

Squarely astride the traditional practices that are still quite solidly with us and the sometimes bewildering kaleidoscope of newer alternatives sits the classroom teacher. In the hands of this very important person lies the real direction the schools will take. It will be his wisdom—or lack of it—that will influence decisions as to which parts of older education will be retained and which areas of new knowledge and skill will be developed in depth and added to the repertoire of teaching and learning.

But decisions of any sort regarding past, present, and

future practices in the organization of curriculum, staff, students, or physical plant will be ineffective if the interactive process of classroom learning is left untouched. Certainly this process has not remained completely static through the years, but change has been slow and unsystematic. A brief look at past and present practices in teaching is presented here to serve as a basis for describing possible alternatives for the future.

Teaching and Learning: Past

Sociologists describe education as a process through which the young of a society are inducted into the culture of the society. Inherent in this notion is the picture of an older and wiser authority controlling and shaping the behavior of an immature group of growing individuals. The degree of rigidity of such behavior control has depended upon the static or dynamic condition of the society at any given time. Thus in ancient societies, such frameworks of education as the Indian Caste System and Plato's Republic grew out of a felt need by its elders to structure the present and future of a society in what seemed to them the best possible way.

Schooling (that part of education conducted in a formalized setting by specialists) began in the context of authority and of the passing on by rote methods of universal truths that could not be questioned by young learners. The teacher knew, and that was why he was the teacher; the learner did not know, and that was why he was the learner. Communication between teacher and learners was one way at a time with the odds heavily weighted on the side of the teacher. First, the teacher would teach by lecturing and demonstrating; then, the learner would recite orally or on paper so that the teacher could determine whether understanding had taken place. Thus the now well-defined roles of teacher and student were developed. The teacher planned, introduced, developed, explained, illustrated, and summarized usually by oral means, though he might use drawings or models from time to time. The listening learner took notes, did individual thinking, and then demonstrated his success or failure to understand, or at least to recite, what he had been taught.

Motivation, concern, interest, need—all these were assumed. If the student lacked any of these, he was weeded out of the system. Proof of learning through test-taking was structured by the demand that the learner repeat the material in the teacher's terms without question. Any questioning or attempt to develop new knowledge was restricted to the mature person who had finished schooling. After years of enforced passive acceptance, however, the mature adult tended to be conditioned to the status quo.

Possibly because of his own conditioning, a man of the twentieth century would be disturbed by such a rote approach to schooling. It is clear, however, that such a world would be satisfying to many people who see the raising of questions as both threatening and difficult. Aldous Huxley, in *Brave New World*,[8] carries this notion of societal and personal security into the psychological setting of the modern world, and George Orwell, in *1984*,[9] goes further into the current notion of brainwashing to exact not only conformity but willing conformity from all citizens.

Even in the Renaissance, where inductive reasoning had taken hold, the experience of Galileo and others demonstrated the generality of violent resistance to change and to new ideas. In the nineteenth century, Semmelweis was driven insane by the refusal of his medical brethren to accept the suggestion that an examining doctor wash his hands. Such resistance came, at least in part, from the schooling practices of the time. Pasteur, with his talk about "little animals which no one could see," highlighted a changing climate in the acceptance of the new. Although he was initially resisted by higher authorities, he was eventually able to win his battle for acceptance in his own lifetime. During the past generation, Jonas Salk was able to put over a program for prevention of polio with only minimum

[8]Huxley, Aldous, *Brave New World*, New York: Harper, 1946. See also by the same author *Brave New World Revisited*, New York: Harper, 1958.
[9]Orwell, George, *1984*, New York: Harcourt, 1949.

resistance. During these centuries, schooling has slowly moved from being a simple mirror of society to acting as an agent for change or at least the acceptance of change.

Teaching and Learning: Present

With the Renaissance came the beginnings of many things: the restructuring of social organizations within the society, the rise of a spirit of inductive inquiry into the physical—and later into the psychological—world, and the gradual development of leisure time for large numbers of the world population. The first of these changes put larger and larger percentages of available young people into schools, the second developed a generalized support for the growth of psychological investigation and support of its findings, the third gave more people time to think about, try out, and evaluate alternatives to the traditional wisdom.

In American schooling, this has led to challenges in a number of areas. Children are seldom currently thought of as little adults. Rather, they are perceived as growing organisms to be heard as well as seen. Even the most authoritarian American teacher must soften his approach or face the evaluation of his students both of what he says and of him as a person. In response to what has been discovered about the needs of young people, an extensive co-curricular program has developed, and teachers in the regular curriculum areas have had to become more conscious of adaptive techniques to "reach" and to "motivate" their students.

Seats have been unscrewed from classroom floors (this is progress even though they may rarely be moved from their traditional places), the teacher's raised platform has all but disappeared, there is a permissive atmosphere (within certain rigid limits), and students are encouraged to question ideas in the now generally approved quest for "critical thinking." Teachers are expected to have good senses of humor, respect of and *for* students, well-developed habits of fair play, and approaches that are perceived as reasonable in students' terms. The modern American teacher must like his students and know them through permissive practices within the classroom, out-of-class encounters where possible, and consultation with parents, permanent records, and guidance counselors.

An ideal toward which today's teacher strives is to be a respected, genial buddy to his students without, of course, going "too far" and inviting behavior problems. He does not order; he requests. He stands at the front of the class in his section of the "egg-crate" school building before thirty youngsters seated in unscrewed, if unmoved, seats in rows one behind the other and waits for their acceptance of the fact that the period has begun. When they recover from their between-period gaiety and face expectantly to the front waiting for the performance called teaching to begin, he asks, "Would you open your books to page twenty-eight?" Rarely raised is the question as to what would happen if they replied, "No, we'd rather not."

Behind the apparently permissive atmosphere, however, lie many aspects of authoritarian control. Most grading of student effort includes evaluation of satisfactory conformity to the teacher's concept of good behavior, schools still use detention rooms, many teachers and principals hold to the belief in practice that the boy may be spoiled if the rod is spared, parents are frequently called in to account for the deviance of their offspring, and suspension and expulsion are always possible if all else seems to fail to bring a student into line with the expectations of a particular school. And these expectations may extend from behavior to appearance. A perfectly docile boy with long hair or a quiet girl with a short skirt may find great pressure being applied by teachers and administrators to put an end to such flouting of the norms of their elders.

In the classroom, youngsters may flout, they may rebel, they may retreat into silence, they may smilingly conform, *but rarely do they have an opportunity to face the problems of intergenerational conflict squarely and to learn more constructive ways of handling it.*[10] Despite this, of course, some do learn to

[10]The recent confrontation on our college campuses and in the streets of our major cities between those under thirty and those over thirty (in fact the whole communications breakdown expressed in the statement, "Don't trust

be self-directing and to cope with problems of authority. Many others, however, go on struggling throughout their later marital and occupational encounters. It becomes more apparent each year that learning to deal creatively with oneself and others is a need at least as pressing as that of coping with the 3 R's. Clever writing alone does not explain the great popularity of books such as Berne's *Games People Play*,[11] which deals with the lack of authentic behavior in adult interaction.

Teachers are beginning slowly to understand that any group setting is packed with human relations needs that have to be met before people can get on with the learning of subject matter. Large numbers of students find the traditional classroom actively harmful to their self-images day after day. Many withdraw physically and become dropout statistics; much larger numbers stay physically while withdrawing psychologically. Still others do not withdraw, but learn to play the highly sophisticated game of teachers and students much in the same way that they role-played cops and robbers at earlier ages. Their real world of personal meaning, where they can authentically play themselves, usually exists *outside* the classroom.

These students have intercommunication problems, and their teachers should be experts in communication. Unfortunately, this facet of teacher preparation has been almost totally ignored until quite recently. Teachers should be—and are to some extent—scholars in their subject disciplines. But teaching is not accomplished by the teachers demonstrating to their students how learned they, the teachers, are. Teaching is accomplished only when learners learn, retain what they learn, and develop both the urge to use their learning in later situations and some methodology for putting learnings to work. If one accepts these criteria, even what seems to be successful learning can be questioned. For example, the pre-service

anyone over thirty.") has strong implications for curriculum review in the schools. Historically, subjects have been taught in the schools bearing on citizenship education. But rarely in the classroom or in the school as a whole has there been any real confrontation of the intergenerational problem. What seems needed is dialogue between teachers and students on the feeling level. If young people can learn to communicate with their elders, we may be spared repetitions of August 1968 in Chicago.

[11]Berne, Eric, *Games People Play*, New York: Grove Press, 1964.

teacher who gets an "A" in psychology and then goes into a class behaving as if he had never studied the subject can be said by his professor who granted the "A" to have learned the subject. But if he does not use his learnings or even think of them in an actual human situation, one might question the value of his having taken such a course in the first place. One answer could be that in many of his college classes, the teacher himself was playing the game of teachers and students.

In order to examine current notions of what teaching and learning is, a look at concepts now accepted in psychology and education is helpful. There is, of course, no guarantee that these notions have been or are being used. If they are not, it may be the ineffective way in which the teacher himself learned them, including the fact that while he may accept some or all, he may not know how to implement them.

The following list is illustrative rather than exhaustive. The student is encouraged to read more deeply in the field and to develop his own basic set of concepts to guide his teaching.

1. Learners (and teachers) bring with them to the classroom a cluster of understandings, skills, appreciations, attitudes, and feelings that have personal meaning to them and are in effect the sum of their reactions to previous stimuli.
2. Learners (and teachers) are individually different in many ways even when ability grouped.
3. Learners (and teachers) have developed concepts of self, which directly affect their behavior.
4. Learning may be defined as a change in behavior.
5. Learning requires activity on the part of the learner. He should not be passive.
6. Learners ultimately learn what *they* actively desire to learn; they do not learn what they do not accept or come to accept.
7. Learning is enhanced when learners accept responsibility for their own learning.
8. Learning is directly influenced by physical and social environment.
9. Learning occurs on successively deeper levels.
10. Learning is deepened when the learning situation provides opportunity for applying learnings in as realistic a situation as is feasible.

11. Learners are motivated when they understand and accept the purposes of the learning situation.
12. Learners are motivated by success experiences.
13. Learners are motivated by teacher acceptance.
14. Learners are motivated when they can associate new learnings with previous learnings.
15. Learners are motivated when they can see the usefulness of the learning in their own personal terms.

Number one refers to what John Dewey wrote concerning the "whole child," and what the present author calls the "whole teacher." These are the hidden ingredients of the interaction process. While they affect everything that goes on in the class, they are usually ignored since the traditional rules of the "teacher and students" game state that everyone must "get down to business" and start covering the ground even before students and teacher develop any personal relationships.

Number two is the old individual differences cliché, which everyone recognizes like they do Mark Twain's weather, but no one does much about. Again, much of the problem here is caused by the almost hysterical urge on the part of many teachers not to waste time. The result of such an urge is a set style and approach to all learners. The possible waste of individual students' time with this approach apparently does not cause the same teacher concern.

Number three, like one and two, is often ignored, mainly because teachers do not know how to handle it and have never received sensitivity training[12] to make them conscious of the

[12]Sensitivity Training, variously referred to as T-Group Training and Basic Encounter Groups, is an attempt to help individuals learn how human groups (as opposed to aggregates) set agendas, develop norms, solve problems, develop patterns of communication, and deal with both affect and cognition in defining and reaching goals. Trainees learn by experiencing how their behavior really affects others, how people can help each other to reduce their need for defensive shields and become more authentic, and how humans can develop a climate of mutual trust.

The technique involves many intensive small group (12–13 persons) experiences usually carried on in a *cultural island* setting away from telephones and the normal daily pressures and distractions. A T-Group begins as an *aggregate*, interacts, studies its own interactions, and gradually matures into a *group*. The framework is one of emotional growth and has the effect, for most participants, of releasing potential and helping people to use their emotions productively rather than hiding behind them. The person who goes through

effects of their personal behavior on that of students. Many teachers, kindly and considerate in other contexts, can be heard to say to visitors (often within hearing range of lower ability grouped students), "These are the dummies. You really should come around during the sixth period and see my good class." Often the most effective learning that a student does is to develop clearly the notion that he is stupid, dirty, and undesirable.

Number four relates to outcome of the classroom experience. It refers to increased ability to deal intelligently with the subject matter and to be able to apply it where it is relevant. In addition, it has to do with attitudes. Sinclair Lewis' Babbitt[13] bragged that his college learnings had never touched him. In *The Corn is Green*,[14] on the other hand, a teacher who was not

---

sensitivity training learns as much as he will allow himself to learn. In addition to dealing more wisely with his own emotions, he develops skills in allowing others to deal with theirs. This is priceless learning for all people, but it is particularly valuable for classroom teachers who have been trained to deal only with the intellects of their students.

Presently, the major source book in this field is Bradford, Leland, ed., *T-Group Theory*, New York: Wiley, 1964. Most universities provide some courses in the dynamics of groups at work, though many of these are still taught by lecture.

Major sources of training programs include:

National Training Laboratories
National Education Association
1201 16th St. NW
Washington, D.C. 20036

Western Behavioral Sciences Institute
1121 Torrey Pines Road
La Jolla, California (92037)

Esalen Institute
Big Sur, California (93920)

At the local levels, university departments of social psychology are usually helpful contacts. The author's own organization is an example of a college based service for consultation and sensitivity training programs for schools, businesses, and community organizations:

Montclair Human Resources Laboratory
Box 457
Montclair State College
Upper Montclair, New Jersey 07043

[13]Lewis, Sinclair, *Babbitt*, New York: Harcourt, 1950.
[14]Williams, Emlyn, *The Corn is Green*, New York: Random House, 1941.

satisfied with merely presenting material made a successful effort to reach a young man who had not been profiting from his learning before his encounter with her. The implication seems to be that the teacher must reach each student before he can begin to teach him. A few teachers just do not care, but others who do are blocked by not knowing *how* to reach students.

Numbers five through fifteen deal directly with the teaching process that develops student motivation. The learner must be active intellectually and physically, he must desire to learn, he must accept the purposes of any specific classroom, he must feel success and the possibility of further success, he must fulfill his social needs of acceptance, achievement, and affection, and he must "see something in it for him" in terms of both immediate and future usefulness of the learning.

A big job? Of course it is. And it requires the development of usable concepts by the teacher. Too often, in the history of teacher education, students have filed such data as these fifteen statements away on their mental shelves as nice, hazy, idealistic things to put into practice when and if they ever get around to them. Thus there has existed, and still exists, a frustrating gap between theory and practice. More effective and more truly professional education will occur only when the teacher sees concepts such as these as stark realities that will not disappear even if one pretends they do not exist. They *do* exist, and they are vital ingredients of schooling that need to take their proper place alongside the equally necessary teacher expertise in subject matter.

Teaching and Learning: Future

All stages of learning ultimately form a composite within the individual learner. For purposes of discussion, however, it is helpful to analyze the process stage by stage in order to deal separately with each component. It should be recognized, of course, that any such analysis must refer to a particular definition of learning. The analysis here infers a certain way of viewing learning that has been suggested by the findings in the social psychology of education for over a generation.

Components of learning within the concept used in this book would include: (1) readiness activities; (2) organizational cognitive processes; (3) feedback of intellectual and emotional response; (4) adjustive cognitive processes; (5) guided application; (6) valuing and internalizing; and (7) summarizing feedback.

One of the first things a class and its teacher will do in the future (and good learning experiences of the past and present have shown awareness of this necessity) will be to carry on activities that will cut through *over*formal, distrustful relationships. The whole child *and* the whole teacher come into the classroom. Each has individual values, attitudes, and characteristic ways of behaving and of perceiving others. As they get to know each other, it becomes less necessary for them to employ irritating behaviors, and even the behaviors themselves become less irritating. When we *know* Charlie or Patricia, we are much more accepting of their behavior. This, in turn, makes it less necessary for us to change their behavior so that they can become more like us. It might be much more helpful to all concerned if they became more authentically *like themselves*.[15]

Normal "entry activity" for all of us, as a group (class) begins, is to test for rules and boundaries. None of us can really relax and be ourselves until we learn, in our own terms, just what is expected of us and how people get treated in this new situation. In most cases, we attempt to learn the rules from observing others. Only forceful, dominating personalities attempt personally to build the norms of the group in its initial

[15] Authenticity is used here in the sense of being spontaneously frank about your feelings in your relations with others. The non-authentic teacher when threatened by two whispering students will use sarcasm or force to stop the threat. The authentic teacher will tell the students, in the class setting, that he feels uncomfortable because they are talking. This second behavior will bring the conflict out into the open where it can be resolved. The first behavior only increases both teacher and student frustration.

On page 153 of a fascinating little book (Jourard, Sidney M., *The Transparent Self*, Princeton, New Jersey: D. Van Nostrand, 1964.) Jourard says, "This entire book can be regarded as an invitation to 'authentic being.' Authentic being means being oneself honestly, in one's relations with his fellows. It means taking the first step at dropping pretence, defenses, and duplicity. It means an end to 'playing it cool,' an end to using one's behavior as a gambit designed to disarm the other fellow, to get him to reveal himself *before* you disclose yourself to him."

moves. In the classroom, the age and authority difference between teacher and students usually puts the teacher, at least
in the beginning stages, in the position of norm setter. But
readiness activities could provide the opportunity *and the responsibility* of norm setting for the students as well as for the
teacher. This process of sharing is a difficult one because it has
not been done traditionally, and both teachers and students
have locked themselves into stereotyped roles. A group-centered norm will not appear just because the teacher smiles and
says, "Let's plan our learning experience together." To overcome years of dependency conditioning (and this includes the
teacher), the group will have to learn first how people work
together. Only then can they effectively plan together.

Such initial learning, while difficult, will pay spectacular
dividends as the aggregate of individuals begins to become a
cohesive group of learners. Once the interaction pattern has
been established so that rules of the game and expectations of
teacher and students are known, the process of cognitive
growth can go on in a more relaxed and enthusiastic atmosphere
with less need for dominating or withdrawal behavior. At this
point, the group is really ready to organize itself for learning
and carrying out inquiry into the discipline under consideration
in this particular class.

The third step would include various ways of checking and
testing the group norms. Have feelings changed? Is everyone
participating freely? Do we need to modify the norms, or do
we have to admit that they never were really accepted by *all*
members? How can we improve the social-emotional climate of
the group?

Integrated with this feedback would be a check on the
understanding of facts, concepts, skills, and other learnings.
Have we learned what we set out to learn? What do we have to
do now? Can we go ahead or do we have to relearn some
material? How can we use what we have done to go further?
What avenues of inquiry have been opened?

Step four is an outgrowth of step three, and consists of
actions taken in response to the questions raised by the feedback. The learning group has now progressed a fair distance on

the road to becoming a mature, self-directing, self-correcting set of individuals. Dependence on the teacher as initiator, lecturer, and sole evaluator has been somewhat lessened, and students are reacting to the responsibility for making the learning a successful experience. Dealing with the data from the feedback process, they have become more able to cooperate with the teacher in planning and carrying out an application experience where they can put their learnings to a test. In arriving at this point, they are able to benefit more fully from the teacher's knowledge and talents. And he himself can play the professional role of intellectual guide and mentor less distracted by the baby-sitting chores that result from a non-cohesive group where the teacher and the students find themselves on opposing sides of an emotional game whose very existence is denied while so-called teaching goes on.

While the application experience of step five proceeds, the sixth step of valuing and internalizing keeps pace. The latter step involves student evaluation of the experience in their own terms—a personal involvement in deciding what is important to them, what can be used, what further learnings are necessary. Put into a more proper perspective is the eventual taking of a test. While the importance of a final grade by no means disappears, the learning becomes even more important. The student has begun to take control and responsibility for evaluation of his own progress both in this class and beyond. His personal values are brought into play and reinforced or modified because he suddenly sees personal meaning in this whole process of education.

Since the course—semester or year—does have a final cut-off, the last days or weeks should be devoted to step seven, a summarizing feedback. This should be a pupil-teacher planned evaluation of the total experience, and it should occupy time enough to make it a meaningful reinforcement of previous learnings.

Traditionally, this process is carried on solely by the teacher, takes place in a brief "final examination," and the results are used only to support a grade on a piece of paper. For the students, the experience is one of regurgitating rather than of learning. Results of testing conducted six weeks or six months later are usually most discouraging.

Since it is inherent in the learning concept used in this book that teacher and students should be concerned with use of the knowledge, skills, and attitudes developed in the course, the summarizing feedback is seen as a final opportunity for learning rather than a teacher spotcheck on student attendance and attention. As a rule of thumb, the process should take at least two weeks for a semester course and three to four weeks for a full year's course.

SUMMARIZATION WITH NO FEEDBACK

It is the fate of a book read by unknown readers in unknown contexts to gain no feedback for its author. He can only hope that even at this stage of presentation there will be an interest in and an opportunity for some feedback from students reading this material to their teacher and from student to student. What is the climate of feeling in your class? What are its norms of behavior? Who set them? How are they tested? Where will you go from here? Will your experiences in this class have personal meaning for your future? What have you done to help your teacher to help you? Is he, in your eyes, a human being or just a convenient scapegoat for your own lack of interest, motivation, creativity, imagination, initiative, or energy?

Since the book cannot receive your responses, it must, like all books, go on to the next chapter. As a final preparation for moving on, however, let us look again at what has been said in this chapter.

It began with the obvious statement that most schooling takes place in a group setting, and went on to note that schooling has been so busy dealing with day-to-day pressures that it has rarely had time to evaluate its processes. The once revolutionary idea that education should be for all has caught up with American schools almost before they were ready. Since they had been in the college preparation business for such a long time, their readiness to deal with other types of students was not highly developed. Failures to reach the non-college bound are easily documented by dropout statistics. Since, in America, the teenage dropout has literally no place to go but the street corner, his leaving the school is a biting criticism. But, while this is a problem, the case of the psychological dropout, less easily documented, should give the highly subject-centered teacher much to think about.

Yet, mere thinking will not solve problems. The traditionally educated teacher has rarely been taught effectively to teach *people*. He, and his professors, have concentrated on the learning of the subject often at the expense of the development of methodology in teaching it. Even the currently new ideas in schooling practices contain little that relates directly to what the teacher does when he is teaching. Much has been written about the organization of team teaching, but little exists that details the *how* of the practice. If current teaching leaves much to be desired, the creation of teams will not, in itself, improve the situation. It is time that new approaches to *interaction* in the classroom were developed and tested. The material in this book should provide at least a small step in this direction.

Past teaching has consisted of authoritarian *telling* by the teacher to a rigidly controlled captive audience. Present teaching is a more permissive *telling* by the teacher to a less rigidly controlled captive audience. Future teachers will do less telling as a one-way process. They will instead focus on the teacher-student and student-teacher interaction and its improvement in both the cognitive and affective domains. Such a focus should result in more freedom, more responsibility, and more learning for all members of the classroom group, including the teacher himself.

2

The Teacher
and the Class:
A Theoretical Framework
for Interaction

IN CHAPTER ONE, the outlines of the book were drawn in broad strokes. It is time to sketch in the details before proceeding to actual teaching operations. Chapter One is an overview of teaching, and Chapter Two is the theory underlying a certain approach to teaching. The remaining chapters will illustrate this approach.

THE THEORY

Because interaction is at the base of the material presented here, and because it is a frequently misunderstood term, a definition at this point is in order.

Human confrontation and communication (meeting and speaking) is a fascinating interplay of subtle assumptions and meanings that most people learn to deal with in a more or less effective fashion. Difficulties arise only when meanings are not clarified or when assumptions are not checked. Such clarifying and checking, however, is not always an easy matter. How, for example, can a sixth-grade boy go about asking his teacher whether or not he really meant to be sarcastic?

There is a communication joke that becomes more profound as one speculates about the hidden meanings and assumptions implied. It involves two psychologists who meet in the lobby of a hotel after breakfast. "Good morning," says Dr. Brown. "I wonder what he meant by that," thinks Dr. Green.

Green's question may be provoked by something perceived in Brown's behavior, or it may be merely that Green is making an unfounded assumption that a hidden meaning exists. If he follows the pattern of most people, however, he will never ask his question aloud except possibly later to a third person. This failure to check, in itself, serves to cloud further communication between the two men, but an even more serious problem can arise. Green may try to get an answer from Brown without actually asking the question. Getting further verbal and non-verbal responses from Brown, he may build on his original assumption that Brown was being unfriendly or mocking or whatever. If Green can convince himself that his assumption is correct (notice that he never really checks it directly), he may take retaliatory action by being nasty to or by ignoring Brown. Meanwhile, Brown may not have felt anything but good will toward Green and be quite puzzled by his nasty response. This puzzlement can turn to anger on Brown's part and a feeling that good will is wasted on the likes of people like Green. Following the unfortunate human habit of failing to check on assumptions, he will probably not ask Green what the trouble is. Instead, Brown may, himself, become nasty, thus assuring Green that he was correct in his original assumption.

In the classroom, a similar miscommunication may occur between teacher and student, and the presence of the other members of the class usually makes things worse. Using the pattern of *Assumption, Intent, Message, Reception,* the interchange might go like this:

JOHNNY: *Message*

Assumption: The teacher appreciates honesty in student responses. He has made this statement in class.

Intent: I'll try telling him what I really think about Beethoven. Maybe he can help me to understand the music. (I'll also show the class that I'm not a square.)

"Mr. Williams, I can't get with this Beethoven character. He doesn't send me anywhere."

TEACHER:

Reception: I really want students to respond and respond honestly, especially Johnny. I feel good that he has finally spoken.

Assumption: He likes and trusts me. He has a good sense of humor. He is familiar with the notion of long hair in connection with classical music.

"Johnny, with your long hair I thought you'd be the first person in the class to appreciate classical music."

Intent: I'll make a joke to show him and the class that I'm not just an old fuddy duddy. This will bring us closer and encourage him toward more class participation.

JOHNNY:

Reception: Oh, oh. What's happening here? The class laughed and I looked like a fool. I feel uncomfortable and a little fearful. That's what I get for trying to play the game straight.

Assumption: Mr. Williams doesn't really want honesty. Also, he doesn't like me or the way I wear my hair. Also, he is a sarcastic so-and-so.

"Well, Mr. Williams, only squares from squaresville like that kind of garbage. Nobody who was a real man would waste his time listening to it. I don't know why we have to study this junk anyway."

Intent: I'll show him. He can't push me around and get away with it. Also, I'll regain my leadership of the class. They won't laugh again.

TEACHER:

Reception: That hurt. He slams the subject just when I have most of the kids motivated. He raises the old questions of the virility of male music teachers. And just when I thought he was coming around and getting interested.

Assumption: Johnny is just a nasty fresh boy. You can't treat his kind with decency—all he understands is force. He is ignorant, he doesn't like me, and he is turning the class against me and the subject.

Intent: I will straighten him out. He must not get away with insolence. It is bad for discipline. I will show him who is boss here.

"We will have no more of that sort of talk, young man. If you can't appreciate good music, the least you can do is to keep quiet and not parade your ignorance. (TO CLASS) Now, the next record we will hear is. . . .

JOHNNY:

Reception: I know I'm not so bright, but it hurts to have the teacher hit me over the head with it.

Assumption: Mr. Williams is really a fraud. He puts on a

nice act, but he's really a
fink just like most teachers.
I tried to be honest, and
now he's really out to get
me.

Intent: I'll keep my mouth shut
from now on, but I won't pay
any attention to this music
junk. It's sort of too bad. I'd
sort of like to know more
about it, but that's out now.
I'll show that so-and-so.

In analyzing the interchange above, several things should
be noted:

1. This is a case of blocked interaction. What will follow with
   the class will not be interaction, but a series of one-way
   actions.
2. Interaction includes feelings and perceptions in addition to
   messages.
3. Interaction occurs only when messages and assumptions of
   the sender's intent are clarified.
4. Socialization norms in the American society act against such
   clarification. Rarely do we check our assumptions directly
   even with close friends.
5. People often react defensively to words without considering
   the person saying them. (Johnny was quick to take offense
   without considering that Mr. Williams might possibly have
   meant his statement as a joke and might be clumsy in expressing himself. Mr. Williams was quick to form a judgment of Johnny without considering that the laughter of
   the class might have hurt Johnny's feelings and that his need
   for peer status was unusually strong.)
6. Effective interaction is difficult before people form relationships and check out some of their initial assumptions about
   each other. (If Johnny had confidence in Mr. Williams'
   generally good intentions, he would not have reacted so
   rapidly without giving the teacher the benefit of the doubt.)
7. A group situation makes initially difficult interaction even
   more so. (It was the laughter of the class that hastened
   Johnny's defensive reaction. It was the thought of the bad
   effect on the class that helped Mr. Williams decide to put

Johnny in his place in an authoritarian manner. And the class itself undoubtedly had varied individual reactions to the interchange that would affect *their* behavior toward Mr. Williams and Johnny in the future.)

Interaction, then, is a process of communication between two or more people where both the linguistic meaning and the emotional response are mutually clarified whenever clarification seems necessary. As is noted in number 6 above, the development of relationships is helpful to effective interaction. This suggests that less need for clarification becomes necessary as more meaningful relationships are formed. With close friends, for example, we do not have to be constantly on guard against misunderstanding. We say that our friends *understand us,* by which we mean that they do not misinterpret our intent even when our language is clumsy. Also, we *understand them,* by which we mean that we trust them and feel that their intent is to be helpful and supportive.

Some of the determinants of interactive situations may be illustrated as follows: Person (A), finding himself in a social situation, wishes to communicate with person (B). Before codifying his message, however, he passes his thoughts through a number of personal "screens." In such screening, he asks himself questions about:

Situation

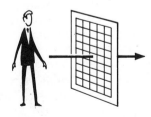

How do I perceive the importance of this situation to me?
What is really expected of me?
What level of language will best reach this audience?
How should I begin?

Self

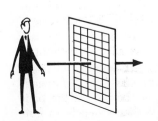

How confident do I feel in this situation?
Is my position superior, peer, inferior?
Am I being evaluated?
Am I really worth anything?
Do these people respect me?
What impression will I make?

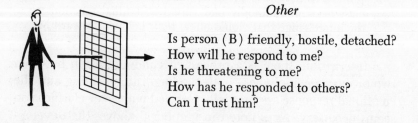

Other

Is person (B) friendly, hostile, detached?
How will he respond to me?
Is he threatening to me?
How has he responded to others?
Can I trust him?

When (A) attempts to communicate with (B), his attempt and his feelings about it are somewhat influenced, in a group situation, by persons (C), (D), (E), (F), (G), and (H). All of these impressions may finally inhibit him to the point of silence even though he wants to say something. He may feel that the risk involved in speaking is too great for him to overcome.

If and when he does speak to (B), (B) and the others receive the message through *their* perceptual screens as in figure 1. (B)'s reply is filtered through *his* screens and comes back to (A) through (A)'s incoming screens. In addition to (B)'s reply, of course, (A) also receives verbal or non-verbal messages from the other members of the group (the laughter of the class while Johnny was speaking to Mr. Williams). All of these messages, some quite problematical and unclear, must

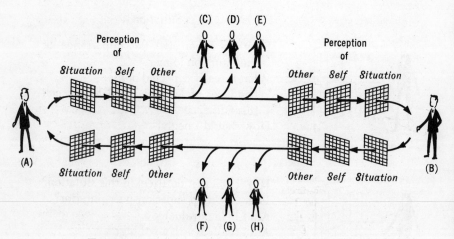

Figure 1. Perceptual Screens in Group Interaction.

be decoded by (A) before he can make a decision to speak again or to remain silent.

In the interaction process, *when it is not blocked,* the people involved get a chance to check on and clarify their initial perceptions. As person (A) sends his message, observes reactions of others, and receives replies, his initial perceptions may change. He may have thought, for example, that no one would be interested in what he had to say. If he perceives, after speaking, that they *are* interested, he will be reinforced and more able to send out further messages. He may also be able to differentiate the cognitive and emotional components of his message. His listeners may indicate interest, but lack of cognitive understanding. The perceived interest will prompt (A) to further efforts to make himself cognitively clear. Side effects are also numbered in the interactions. Person (G), for example, may have been inhibited, but seeing the success of (A), may be prompted to try a message of his own.

The notion of interaction, then, includes both emotional and cognitive communication. What is too often ignored in classroom operation is the emotional component. Until a person is at ease (gets to *know* the others), he will not be able to concentrate fully on the cognitive component of the communication process. If person (A) speaks to (B), and (D) laughs, followed by a sarcastic reply from (B), then (A) may be less inclined to speak again. The sensitive teacher will help students to deal helpfully with each other; the insensitive teacher will merely wonder why (A) has become so quiet and urge him to speak up.

Sensitivity and *knowing each other* can be developed in the classroom, and its value to the learning of the subject is great.[1] Such conditions by no means suggest that everyone tiptoe about the classroom, fearful of expressing any negative feel-

---

[1]For one of the classics in classroom student-centered teaching see Cantor, Nathanial, *The Dynamics of Learning,* Buffalo, N.Y.: Foster and Stewart, 1946. For adaptations of non-directive counseling in the classroom setting see Rogers, Carl R., *Client-Centered Therapy,* New York: Houghton-Mifflin, 1965 (Chapter IX, "Student-Centered Teaching," pp. 384–428). For a probing look at the learning of improved group membership behavior see Miles, Matthew B., *Learning to Work in Groups,* New York: Bureau of Publications, Teachers College, Columbia University, 1959.

ings. Rather, it opens the way for dealing with negative reactions in a helpful manner. After all, friends often disagree, but they remain friends. Where interaction is blocked, people treat each other in a formal, ritualistic manner or avoid contact altogether. Where it is unblocked, people get to know each other, there is less need for careful screening, and problems that do occur are dealt with. In a cohesive group, the laughter of (D) and the sarcastic reply of (B) would be clarified and dealt with there and then. Others would come in to support (A) and to mediate between (A) and (B). There would also be opportunity for (D) to clarify the meaning of his laughter. The point is that, even under difficult conditions, the interaction would not stop, and people would not keep their reactions hidden. They would, instead, bring out the feelings and deal with them before going on.

There seem to be two important reasons for working to produce a cohesive group (getting to know, trust, and feel for each other).

First, people tend to work toward their potential in a warm, supportive setting where they can concentrate on learning without too much worry about their social needs. While learning may take place in a cold, formal setting, it is not often very efficient in terms of depth or retention. Without group cohesion many children do not respond openly, and the teacher is forced to persuade, coax, or threaten to get student participation. A warmer, more informal setting does not magically make a fast learner out of a slow learner, but it gives more assurance that each student will be motivated to work up to his individual level of competence.[2]

Second, the building of a cohesive group, which is a challenging learning situation in itself, teaches students to be more

[2]People have always been able to learn facts and concepts without warmth, but they also learn to be remote. Since evidence is conflicting and behavioral outcomes of teaching are rarely measured, perhaps teachers need to experiment and test their objectives more than they do. As used here, warmth implies gentleness, respect, and consideration as opposed to harshness, domination, and disregard of needs and feelings. The teacher who defines warmth as a soupy permissiveness that demands no student effort or performance should check his own attitudes toward self and others.

self-directing happier human beings. In actuality, the "Let's get down to business—no nonsense—be quiet and pay attention—we have to cover the ground" approach of many teachers is a self-defeating travesty of professional teaching. It is based on fearful inhibition that makes the teacher and the students less human than they might otherwise be. It is a request that students suspend all social needs (acceptance, achievement, affection) because these have nothing to do with *serious* class work. The stubborn fact remains that students cannot do such a thing even if they can be persuaded to try.

THE FRAMEWORK

True interaction produces a cohesive classroom group where teacher and students share responsibility for the defining, carrying out, and evaluating of the learning experience. Set forth as an ideal, this sounds exciting and valuable; seen against the background of twenty-five to thirty youngsters in a typical school setting, the ideal seems a difficult one to reach. *And it is.* But the traditional alternative of maintaining an aggregate of non-communicating individuals from September to June seems an even more difficult situation.

Creation of a group by a collection of individuals releases the creative potential of the total membership. The business of teaching and learning does not become easier (it is one of the most difficult of human enterprises), but the abrasive little problems of motivation and discipline largely disappear. The students unite with the teacher to get the job done, which is much more satisfying than the situation where the teacher tries to do the whole thing all by himself.

Sound good? Fine. But how to accomplish it? As a first step there is need for a usable theory that details necessary conditions and sets ground rules for action.

Building Blocks

In building a theory of interaction, it is necessary to deal with three basic factors: (1) the initial human situation, (2) subsequent activities, and (3) outcomes.

Watson[3] conceptualizes these ingredients of an input-output system as STRUCTURE–PROCESS–ATTITUDE. He sees the society as a whole made up of a number of social systems, each having its own generally accepted (by the people involved) STRUCTURE. This STRUCTURE determines the relative positions of persons within the system, and since each position includes the appropriate position behavior, those occupying each position (somewhat like chess pieces) know what they can (should) and cannot (should not) do as long as they are members of that particular group.

When individuals act (and they act according to the behavioral expectations that accompany each position), their actions make up the PROCESS of the system. The playing out of the PROCESS develops generalized ATTITUDES in the participants. Thus a father, acting in accord with the culturally determined STRUCTURE of the family, comes to feel that this is the way a father should act. He may also feel that this is the natural way *all* fathers should act.

The family is the earliest social system experienced by most people. In American homes, the STRUCTURE of the family may include the father as breadwinner, the mother as housekeeper, the children as ornaments differentiated as to position by age and sex, and possibly one or more grandparents who have relinquished their earlier supreme authority in the system and now are seen as burdens to be carried.

This STRUCTURE is diagrammed in Figure 2 with PROCESS indicated by relative size of symbols and direction of arrows. Here, the father is supreme ruler, with mother subordinate and close, and grandfather subordinate and further removed. The children, also subordinate, tend to form a subsystem with the oldest as ruler.

In defining position behavior, it is assumed and accepted (a group norm) that father will make major decisions, that mother will act to support him, that grandfather will have little to say, that the sons will be obedient and submissive, and that the oldest son will act like the father in minor decisions affecting the subsystem of sons that he directs.

[3]These notions are explored in depth in Watson, Goodwin, *Social Psychology: Issues and Insights*, Philadelphia: J. B. Lippincott, 1966, pp. 189–213.

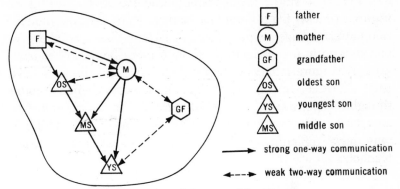

Figure 2. Social System: The Family.

In addition to behavioral norms, STRUCTURE would include spatial configuration and territories. Father and mother would occupy the largest bedroom, the oldest son would have his own room, the two remaining sons would share a room, and grandfather would sleep on a folding bed in the living room. All this territory occupation would flow with STRUCTURE, would develop individual and group activities, and would influence individual and group attitudes toward self and others.

While various members, from time to time, may resist the PROCESS, they accept the STRUCTURE because they know no other and assume that it is natural to mankind. Their ATTITUDES develop from their behavior, which itself has developed from the expectations surrounding the position they occupy. And these attitudes will have great persistence even when they go outside the family into other systems. Thus, the son of an authoritarian father may have difficulty relating to a permissive teacher.

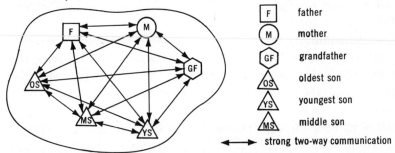

Figure 3. Social System: The Family.

Figure 3 suggests the same basic situation existing in Figure 2, but with a different STRUCTURE. Here, the communication pattern brings people in on a more equal basis, with everyone sharing in major decisions though father and mother have somewhat more influence than grandfather, and the sons have least influence. In this STRUCTURE, the PROCESS demands more thought, responsibility, and self-direction from the participants, and the ATTITUDE outcomes are different. One of *these* children may have difficulty relating to an extremely authoritarian teacher.

Structure, Process and Attitude in the Classroom

Transferring this framework (SPA) to the classroom as a social system, as in Figure 4, one can see the physical and psychological aspects of the traditional situation. Its STRUCTURE includes thirty students seated in rows facing the teacher, who has a larger desk and chair, stands at the front, and may, in some cases, have a raised platform on which to stand. He is, of course, generally bigger, older, and more knowledgeable in the given subject matter. All, or almost all, communication flows through him, and he makes most decisions as to PROCESS, including what will be done, where it will be done, how it will be done, when it will be done, and by whom it will be done.

The students, for the most part, act in response to his cues. From this response—even when negative—they develop ATTITUDES and reinforce the norms of position behavior that are inherent in the STRUCTURE. The teacher plans—the students obey without question except for clarification; the teacher lectures—students take notes; the teacher tests—the students take exams; the teacher evaluates—the students wait to find out whether or not they learned anything.

Changing the STRUCTURE, as in Figure 5, changes PROCESS (though it will take many students some time to get used to the change) and eventually changes ATTITUDES. In this changed STRUCTURE, the students have more responsibility. They talk to each other as well as to the teacher, all communication does not have to flow through the teacher, and there is more student participation expected in terms of planning, executing, and evaluating.

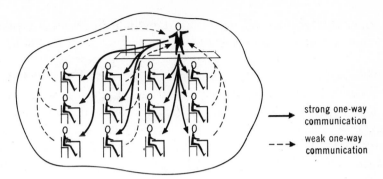

strong one-way
communication

weak one-way
communication

Figure 4. Social System: The Classroom.

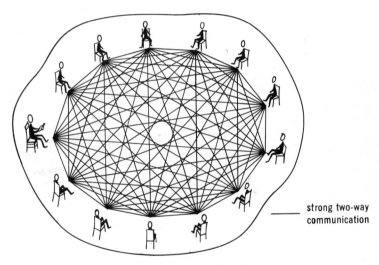

strong two-way
communication

Figure 5. Social System: The Classroom.

In the cohesive learning group, the teacher by no means relinquishes control or ultimate responsibility.[4] Rather, he shares these with the students as junior partners or apprentices and teaches them how to respond in this more democratic situa-

---

[4]For an exploration of the concept of status-leader behavior in the group setting see Gorman, Alfred H., *The Leader in the Group,* New York: Bureau of Publications, Teachers College, Columbia University, 1963. Probably one of the greatest blocks to democratic teaching is the teacher's fear that he will lose control and respect. This fear is a real one and cannot be dismissed lightly. But it should not block action. In the creation of a cohesive learning group, the teacher changes his role from dominance to guidance; *he does not merely abandon his class to their own devices.*

tion. His behavior changes from dictator to that of most valuable of many group resources.

The Framework

At this point in the theory development there are three main areas though specific terms vary:

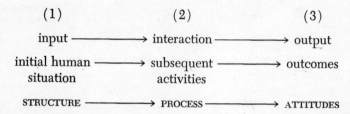

With these factors as background, it is possible to construct a framework for understanding, using, and testing the procedures outlined in the chapters to follow.[5] Figure 6 details the essential parts of this theory of classroom interaction. To the basic input–interaction–output, a process of feedback has been added, and each of the four resulting factors has been defined more specifically. They are:

I
INITIAL SITUATION

(a)	(b)
Participant Background	*Group Structure*
Knowledge, understandings, skills, attitudes, appreciations, self-concepts, and ways of reacting to people which the teacher and his students have at the beginning of the course.	Initially accepted norms of behavior for teacher and students. Accepted procedures such as teacher planning, use of basic text, homework, oral class recitation, test-taking, raising hands for attention, seating arrangements, and general student immobility for the class period. Time and place of class meetings.

---

[5]While the chapters following deal with the growth of affect in students as distinguished from their cognitive growth, teaching and learning in either of

II

ACTIVITIES

(c)

Interaction

Verbal (and non-verbal by means of facial expression and body attitudes) communication between teacher and students and among students.

(d)

Theory Input

Concepts underlying the process of human communication presented by teacher and/or students *after* interaction has taken place, the purpose being to increase personal insight into what is going on and into how it may be analyzed and improved.

III

FEEDBACK

(e)

Data Gathering

Teacher and student feelings about the effectiveness and satisfaction of the interactive process in the classroom. Instruments, in addition to general discussions, include reaction sheets, questionnaires, agree-disagree exercises, opinionnaires, and sociograms.

(f)

Data Analysis

Use of both theory (d) and gathered data (e) to check the effectiveness of present interaction and to suggest ways of improving the process or of retesting apparently successful activities. Students as well as the teacher are involved in doing this analysis.

---

these domains can be conceptualized in this framework. In this book, the framework will be used for activities that involve emotions and human relationships. It cannot be overemphasized, however, that *both* these domains merge in the classroom. A focus on affect does *not* mean the exclusion of cognition. And the opposite is equally true. The most authoritarian cognitive-centered teacher cannot really exclude affect even if he tries. If this is a valid statement, teachers need to deal with affect rather than try to pretend it is not present and that it does not affect learning.

IV

EMERGING SITUATION

(g)	(h)
Change in Participant Background	*Change in Group Structure*
Changes in knowledge, understandings, skills, attitudes, appreciations, self-concepts and ways of reacting to people on the part of both teacher and students.	Changes in initial group norms regarding teacher behavior, student behavior, physical arrangements, and procedures.

It is important to note at this point that the interactions referred to in the framework are *not* activities carried out *in addition to* ordinary teaching and learning procedures. They *are* these ordinary procedures to which the elements of analysis, evaluation, and retesting has been added. In the traditional class, these elements are already applied to the cognitive aspects of learning. The theory above suggests that this is not enough to foster a good learning situation. Noting that cognitive aspects are interwoven with affective, or emotional, aspects, it calls for a better balance in dealing with these co-factors than has existed historically in the school.

Since even the most traditional classroom includes some interaction and group growth, the framework is useful in any schooling situation. To the usual class setting, it introduces a focus on three vital elements: (1) the initial and emerging attitudinal and feeling tone of the learning group, (2) the notion of affect feedback, and (3) the use of situation change analysis to affect ongoing activities.

Such a set of procedures can serve to highlight for both teacher and students what is excellent, what is merely good, and what is poor in any teaching approach. In addition, it provides ways of creatively dealing with interaction problems as they are identified.

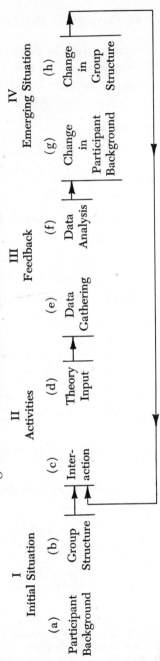

Figure 6. A theoretical framework for classroom interaction.

I		II			III		IV	
Initial Situation		Activities			Feedback		Emerging Situation	
(a)	(b)	(c)	(d)	(e)	(f)	(g)	(h)
Participant Background	Group Structure	Inter-action	Theory Input	Data Gathering	Data Analysis	Change in Participant Background	Change in Group Structure

Cycling Process. Changes affect further activities, and feedback points the way to further change.

AIMS OF IMPROVED CLASSROOM INTERACTION[6]

Before leaving the theory and proceeding to methodology, it would seem helpful to specify some of the aims that prompt professional teachers to take the time to improve interaction in the classroom. What is sought . . .

. . . in the area of teaching and learning is:

a movement from:	toward:
teacher domination	teacher as special member of group
teacher as sole leader	group-centered shared leadership
extrinsic control in hands of teacher	intrinsic control in hands of individuals (including teacher)
active membership of teacher plus two or three verbal students	active membership of total group
stress on subject with exclusion of personal social needs	stress on both cognitive *and* affective elements
almost total dependence on teacher as planner, initiator, and evaluator	student self direction and independence
formal recitation by small percentage of students	spontaneous participation by all
selective inattention by students	careful listening with feedback checks
an aggregate of non-cohesive individuals	a cohesive group of interacting individuals
student learning with the intent of test passing and grade getting	student learning to satisfy personal needs to know and to grow

[6]For a formulation of objectives drawn from a similar framework of learning see Association for Supervision and Curriculum Development, *Perceiving, Behaving, Becoming,* Yearbook, Washington, D.C.: The Association, 1962 ("Signs of Creative Teaching," p. 237).

. . . in the area of emotional growth is:

a movement from:	toward:
guarded, hidden feelings	a norm of openness and spontaneous expression of feelings
unchecked assumptions	positive feelings that assumptions should be checked
neutral feelings toward the meaningfulness of the learning experience	positive feelings that the experience has personal meanings and values
neutral feelings toward the class group	positive, warm response toward others ("my group" feeling).
vague student anxiety: "Who am I in this group?"	personal security: "I am I, accepted and valued
preoccupation with self and with projection of "good" self-image	sensitivity to verbally and non-verbally expressed needs of others
student fear of speaking in a group situation	confidence in expressing feelings, knowledge, and direction
view of teacher as non-human object	view of teacher as human being with feelings similar to those of students

PUTTING THE THEORY TO WORK

Having dealt with the theory and with some of the aims connected with it, we can now proceed to practice. In the following chapters, the intent is to present detailed plans for developing classroom interaction, extending and deepening the process, evaluating activities, and feeding the evaluation back into the circular process inherent in the framework. And finally, since any text is only a beginning for the imaginative teacher, guidelines are suggested for the student who wishes to create approaches and exercises specifically suited to his personal needs.

3

Classroom
Interaction
Processes

ANY APPROACH TO working with groups should begin with a concept of what groups are all about, move on to formulate general objectives concerning ultimate goals, and finally specify specific objectives underlying the particular approach being currently applied. These beginning concerns are what this chapter is all about.

INTERNAL GROUP VARIABLES

In order to understand and put to use the framework of Figure 6, one must be clear as to what happens when an aggregation of individuals (not yet a group) assembles for the purpose of working together (e.g., a tenth-grade history class). Each aggregate faces a similar set of problems as they begin their operations. They must, out of their individual backgrounds and perceptions plus their mutual activity, create a process for communicating plus norms for determining what individual behaviors they will accept and which they will reject. In doing this, they may or may not employ skill, and they may or may not increase the beginning level of skill of the members. The sum total of these efforts and the perceptions of members concerning the efforts creates the group-feeling tone, which is usually termed atmosphere or climate. These variables, comprising sections I and II of the Figure 6 framework, may be listed as follows:

Internal Group Variables[1]

1. Membership
2. Climate or Atmosphere
3. Communications Network
4. Accepted ways of Behaving
5. Communication Skills[2]

Membership

One of the most frequently told school anecdotes concerns the teacher who has a great success in one of his classes—a smooth satisfying experience where everything goes well, everyone participates, and there is a general feeling of good will and accomplishment. Glowing with the realization 'that teaching can be a glorious experience, the teacher walks into a second class, behaves in precisely the same way, and the whole operation falls flat.

This situation seems to occur often enough to deserve serious attention. Looking past the sea of faces turned in various states of attention toward the teacher, an observer can see a host of differing personalities, each formed by heredity and personal reactions to environment past and present. Given these types of individual differences plus a teacher response solely in terms of subject matter presentation and corrective disciplinary control, it is not strange that free, open communication is blocked in so many classrooms. Yet openness and personal

[1]*External* group variables would include the general cultural values, the varied and conflicting values of the immediate community, general expectations of schooling, and the specific expectations of the specific school. While these variables are most significant in their influence on the group, they are outside the scope of the present material, which has its focus on the group as a group.

[2]With regard to any listing of this sort, the reader is encouraged to put the items in his own words and think beyond the descriptions employed in the book. The serious student will see any such listing as a beginning to which he can and should bring his own experience and insights plus further reading in the field.

meaning does occur occasionally, as in the instance of the anecdote. Where the teacher makes his error is in supposing that his actions alone caused the positive situation. If this were true, then he would have no trouble in transferring the wonderful moment to any or all of his other classes. But members vary from group to group, and this quality is a vital ingredient of the learning situation.

Involved closely with differing personalities of members are differing attitudes and expectations toward both self and situation. Does the teacher really know these aspects of his students? Do his students know each other in these terms? How can such knowing affect behavior? In what direction? What would be the result of ignoring student expectations? Can initial expectations be changed? These are pressing questions for the teacher.

Beyond personalities, attitudes, and expectations, but closely connected with them, is the perception of group status. Each member of any group seeks clarification of his individual place in the total scheme. He asks: Who am I in this group? What do people expect of me? What power, if any, do I have? How free can I be to express my real feelings? Do other members respect me? Who will support me? Who will really understand? Whom can I turn to? These are important questions to each student, and when they are not clearly defined they often lead to withdrawal, deviant behavior, clique formation, and/or resistance to teacher direction.

To summarize, membership is a variable based upon what each individual brings with him to a group and what happens to him and to others as a result of his being there.

Climate or Atmosphere

Among the many criticisms of administrators (and these abound joyously in the folklore of schooling) is the description of the principal who prowls the halls expecting all classes to be "quiet and orderly" and woe to the careless teacher who is found sitting on his desk. Many present educators can remember the time when children were compelled to clasp their hands before them on their desks, and each chair was secured firmly to the floor to prevent any disruptive student movement which might break the semi-religious aura of "good behavior" and "serious teaching."

To such restrictive atmospheres, the Progressive Educators of the 1920's brought a sharp reversal in terms of permissiveness and child-centeredness. Hands were unclasped, and even gross body movements were allowed while students were asked what *they* wanted to learn. In some cases, this abrupt removal of rigid structure from above resulted in warm, happy atmospheres where people sought learning without being driven to it; in other situations, unhappy chaos resulted. The restrictive, the warm, happy, the chaotic climates are seen in clear outlines in Lewin's study of the results of Authoritarian, Democratic, and Laissez-faire leadership.[3]

Of course, the attitudes of the members (always including the teacher as member extraordinary) have a great deal to do with the type of climate developed by a classroom group. Endless arguments concerning over-traditional versus soupy progressive teacher approaches do not really end by clarifying anything. More to the point is the realization that members develop climates similar to those with which they have become familiar. The sensitive teacher, schooled in group processes, will help the group to assess the prevailing climate, leaving the way open for change if it seems desirable to most members.

On the other hand, such assessment combined with a notion of freedom of decision arouses a fear reaction in some teachers. Such fears usually act to cut communication and substitute a "Let's pretend that everything's fine" game. Concerns

[3]Lippitt, Ronald and Ralph K. White, "An Experimental Study of Leadership and Group Life," in Eleanor E. Maccoby, Theodore M. Newcomb, and Eugene L. Hartley, *Readings in Social Psychology*, Third Edition, New York: Henry Holt and Co., 1958. Reactions of participants vary somewhat according to previous experiences and individual needs to be dependent or ability to be independent. Democratic leaders stimulated independence twice as much as did Laissez-faire leaders and eight times as much as did Authoritarian leaders. Democratic leader allowed group inquiry and group decision, but was more active as a member than was the Laissez-faire leader. Authoritarian leader was aloof and made most decisions without consulting participants. When leaders arrived late, the Authoritarian-led groups had shown little self-direction in getting anything started; the Laissez-faire groups were active, but not productive; the Democratic groups were both active and productive, showing little need to wait to be told what to do.

over control of students sometimes results in the "Don't smile until Christmas to show 'em who's boss" syndrome. A similar but more subtle response to the fear that students will when given free choice always choose aimless play over rigorous learning leads to the "No nonsense—we have to cover the ground" approach. (It should be noted that not all students are ready for democratic procedures in the classroom. Many actively fear and resist personal freedom and responsibility, thus making the work of the progressive teacher a challenge indeed.)

In any case, a climate is developed as people spend time together and break through the initial formal "ice breaking" period. More often than not, freedom of expression does not develop in the classroom so that the atmosphere develops out of unchecked assumptions and unstated or unclearly stated desires and expectations. It is true that time helps an aggregate become more of a group. No aggregate becomes a group during its first few sessions regardless of the techniques employed. But more than time is needed. No aggregate becomes a group *merely* because of the passage of time.

If a highly formal classroom atmosphere persists, it can lead to tenseness and produce indifference, suspicion, clique formation, inhibition of cognitive as well as emotional responses, and finally result in frustration for all concerned.

The development of an informal climate on the other hand can lead to group loyalty, a feeling of mutual trust, freedom of expression on both cognitive and emotional levels, total group cohesion, and finally satisfaction by all concerned. (Note: at this point, the reader should automatically include the teacher in the word *all.*)

Proof that each group is a product of its particular members lies in the fact that formal and informal atmospheres do not automatically produce the results suggested in the preceding paragraphs. People can be productive in formal settings and quite uncomfortable in relaxed climates. The professional teacher avoids the semantic trap of playing games with words like formal and informal and works with his aggregate to produce a climate that acts optimally to satisfy both social and cognitive needs (always including his own).

To summarize, climate or atmosphere is a variable produced by the expectations of members modified by their perceptions of the present situation and their degree of interaction and communication.

Communications Network

Studies by Hughes[4] and others have found that typical American teacher behavior is *telling*, and that typical American student behavior is *listening*. This notion of teaching as telling is reinforced by the egg-crate school, the rows of student desks, the larger teacher desk, and the teacher's position at the front of the room. Given this traditional and rarely questioned setting, it should not come as a surprise that American classrooms resemble a "story hour" rather than a working group.

Place a teacher at the head of rows of seated, listening students, and the communication pattern resembles Figure 4. Seat everyone in a circle or in a series of circles and the network changes. As in the instance of group atmosphere, however, the mere physical change of seats does not significantly alter the way communication takes place in a classroom. What *is* important is what group members *do* when the physical arrangement is changed. Many teachers skim through a book on group processes, circle their students, and continue to lecture. Or students sit in a series of circles helplessly wasting time until the teacher comes over and tells them what to do. The teacher (who traditionally has done most of the communicating) must accept the responsibility for teaching students how to communicate in various settings if he is to change the network or flow of messages in his classroom.

Aspects of the prevailing network in any group include ways in which people participate and the freedom people feel in contributing ideas. These aspects also affect the kind of participation. Do students merely answer teacher questions?

[4]Hughes, Marie, et al. *Development of the Means for Assessment of the Quality of Teaching in Elementary Schools.* Salt Lake City: University of Utah, 1959. See also Bellack, Arno A. et al. *The Language of the Classroom: Meanings Communicated in High School Teaching.* U.S. Department of Health, Education and Welfare, Office of Education, Cooperative Research Project no. 1497. New York: Institute of Psychological Research, Columbia University, 1963.

Do they speak freely to each other? Do they elaborate, clarify, summarize, and otherwise help the verbal interaction, or are these functions mostly left to the teacher? Does the teacher do most of the talking? Are there efforts to support and encourage members to participate? Is the prevailing network ever analyzed or questioned? Is anything done to improve conditions?

To summarize, the communication network is instrumental in determining the type and amount of participation and interaction in a classroom. It raises the question of who talks to whom, with what intent, and with what result.

Accepted Ways of Behaving

Group norms of behavior are usually spelled out explicitly only in laboratory programs such as science, industrial arts, home economics, fine arts, music, and physical education. They are implicit in teacher behavior toward discipline problems in the regular classroom setting. Spelling out is usually in terms of a list of don'ts developed by the teacher, and it is prompted by dangers inherent in the relative freedom of movement of a laboratory setting.

In some cases, student councils attempt to formulate codes of behavior for the school as a whole, and in the regular classroom the teacher usually indicates what behavior is allowable and what is outlawed. Almost never is the student group, as a group, involved in such decision-making in a direct manner.

Despite this lack of involvement, however, the students do act to set group norms. Thus, in some teachers' rooms, a usually well behaved class may begin to misbehave as a group. As a matter of fact, uniting against a particular teacher is one of the most unifying experiences in the school situation. "We got Mr. Williams to explode in fifteen minutes yesteday. Let's see if we can break our own record today."

Writers such as Coleman[5] have described the peer culture in the schools, and it seems a force to be reckoned with, yet

<hr />

[5]Coleman, James S. *The Adolescent Society: The Social Life of the Teenager and its Impact on Education.* New York: Free Press, 1961. A look at the values of students, which often conflict and rarely connect with the values of their teachers. Interesting insight into a peer culture.

teachers untrained in this area tend to avoid the problem by pretending that nothing is really going on in the class but the teaching of mathematics or whatever. Peer norms certainly seem to affect individual dress and attitudes, and in more subtle ways, they affect classroom behavior. It may be the unspoken notion in Mr. Brown's class that a student who participates is apple polishing, and apple polishing is forbidden. Thus, those students who wish to ask questions, give information, or make comments are inhibited unless they feel that they can stand alone against the sanctions employed by their fellow students.

While the teacher, as appointed leader, acts to impose certain norms, emerging leadership on the part of one or more students also can exert effective pressure. The present writer observed an instance of this while visiting a student teacher who had been assigned a "problem" class. One tall student who sat in the front seat nearest the door apparently did a good deal of the class management with non-verbal signs. He had aligned himself, for the day at least, on the side of the student teacher and was determined that the class would behave itself. As the lesson went on, various individuals and cliques began irrelevant behavior which could have grown into incidents calling for disciplinary action. The student leader knew his group, however, and a glance or frown or slight hand gesture cut off each potential explosion. At the end of the class, the student teacher glowed. "Problem class, bah," she said, "All they need is a businesslike approach and an interesting lesson."

This anecdote does not depreciate in any way the need for a teacher's being interesting and businesslike, but it does highlight the norm-developing potential of groups and the influence of emerging leadership. In the spate of materials and "crash programs" that have focussed on the "gifted child" following the Russian orbiting of Sputnik I, the idea of the "gifted student leader" who might benefit by specific instruction and guided experiences has been largely unexplored. Whether or not such specific programs get off the ground in the near future, it would seem that present teachers could benefit by understanding and making use of peer leadership and peer pressures rather than ignoring them or opposing them.

To summarize, generalized knowledge of accepted ways of behaving is essential as an aggregate extends itself through time. While the most overt expression of norms, at least in the early stages, comes traditionally from the teacher, much influence is exercised by the other group members and the emerging student leaders. Where communication is unclear, generalized group norms are difficult to develop and cliques may form or the class may unite against the teacher. It would seem reasonable to assume that the effectiveness of a group norm increases in proportion to the number of people involved in producing it. The effectiveness of a teacher-made rule is dependent upon the willingness of the student group to accept it and to help enforce it.

Communication Skills

The sender's intent, his assumptions, his message, and its reception are dealt with in Chapter two. Awareness of the difficulties involved in effective communication is an important first step, but the development of verbal skills demands the deepening of awareness plus practice. Such skills include listening, clarifying, testing consensus, problem diagnosis, and the general refinement of ability to convey one's ideas to others in the way one intends them to be received.[6]

In the formation of a group out of the beginning aggregate, member skill is a vital consideration. Too often, teachers attempt a "democratic approach" without thinking of or accepting the responsibility for helping students to gain the verbal interpersonal skills necessary to operate a classroom democracy. It is not enough for the teacher to announce that, "This is going to be a class where we plan together and work together." Having been manipulated in the past, they may not easily trust teachers. But even when students accept such a teacher statement at face value, they may feel inadequate to respond to such a proposal. In order really to plan and work with the teacher they will have to have or develop skills in discussion participa-

---

[6] With reference to the conveying of one's ideas, see the discussion on pp. 23–26 of this book.

tion, ways of distributing responsibilities for work to be done, and ways of problem-solving, decision-making, and evaluating what they have done. Before taking away the comfortable crutch of teacher domination, the professional teacher (providing that he really desires to share the leadership and responsibility in a democratic manner) will begin, with his students, to build communication skills so that the group may move forward in terms of efficiency and satisfaction.

To summarize, communication skills involve verbal interactions that get across individual messages in the way the senders intend them, and that encourage the participation of the total membership in the work of the group.

Internal Group Variables

1. Membership:
    Personalities
    Attitudes
    Expectations
    Perceptions of relative status

2. Climate or Atmosphere:
    Perceptions by group members on a continuum between feelings of:

    Formality ———————— and—Informality
    Tenseness ———————— and—Relaxation
    Indifference ———————— and—Loyalty
    Suspicion ———————————— and — Trust
    Inhibition ———————————— and — Freedom of
    Expression
    Isolation and clique formation — and — Total Group
    Cohesion
    Frustration ———————————— and — Satisfaction

3. Communication Network:
    Who talks to whom?
    Who leads?
    Who follows?
    Is leadership shared?
    Who is quiet or withdrawn?
    Is everyone involved?
    Is there concern to involve all members?
    Who expresses this concern?
        Only the teacher?

Is the major pattern:
 (a) Teacher ──────────→ Students?
 (b) Teacher ←────────→ Students?
              Student
 (c) Teacher ⟋⟍⟋⟍ Student
       Student ⟍⟋ Student

4. Accepted Ways of Behaving:
   Individual expectations
   Individual needs
   Norm development
       by teacher
       by students
       by teacher and students
5. Communication Skills:
   Diagnosing problems which block the group
   Listening
   Involving non-participators
   Clarifying and elaborating ideas
   Giving recognition and support
   Summarizing
   Keeping discussion on track
   Consensus testing
   Harmonizing group issues
These skills are used in specific group tasks such as:
   Planning
   Agenda setting
   Distribution of responsibilities
   Problem-solving
   Decision-making
   Meeting members' personal social needs
   Evaluating in process and as a culminating activity

These five sets of variables are interlocking and at times overlapping. They occur in every classroom setting, though group members rarely seem to understand them clearly or seek to make them explicit. Once they are identified and discussed by the group, however, there is a sharp increase in member feelings of reality as opposed to game-playing-until-the-bell-rings. When an aggregate is able to bring perceptions out into the open so that they can be dealt with, it is on its way to becoming a group. The first step in the analysis and understanding of the group situation is up to the teacher (appointed leader), and he himself needs understanding and the tools of analysis before he can take that first step.

The reader as teacher (appointed leader) is urged to do three things at this point: (1) reread the foregoing material on internal group variables and attempt to put the information in his own terms for the purpose of understanding, (2) add variables that occur to him (why not write in the book?), and (3) check the group-variables material against the framework on page 39. This framework begins with the background the members (always including the teacher) bring to the beginning sessions of the aggregate plus the physical and psychological structure that they also bring based on previous experiences. The theory of learning is contained in the cyclical process of activities, feedback, emerging situation, further activities, further feedback, deepening of the emerging situation, further activities, further feedback, and so on, with the group situation becoming increasingly more clear, more productive, and more satisfying.

ULTIMATE GOALS

Though he may give lip service to a variety of idealistic statements of schooling purposes, a teacher's ultimate goals will flow from his own perceptions and attitudes. If he has received a good traditional education, he will more than likely enter the classroom not having worked out his teaching goals in any great depth. In general, he will want his students to learn the subject he will teach (this goal may mean a number of things according to how deeply he really knows his subject and how he personally defines learning), and he will want them to exhibit "good behavior" while they are doing it (and "good behavior" is certainly a relative term).

The interaction framework that underlies the methodology in this book views cognitive and emotional learning as interdependent. It calls for the analysis of the human factors of the learning group by the human beings involved in order to create a readiness and a methodology for dealing with the subject matter under consideration. Student (and teacher) learnings (yes, the teacher can learn in the classroom) begin in the area of group interaction and *then* move to the area of mathematics, foreign language, home economics, or whatever. This approach differs from the traditional teaching-learning situation, which treats the realities of human expectations, needs, and attitudes as if they did not exist. The theory does not, in any way, move away from a concentration on subject matter and ground to be covered. Rather, it seeks the help of all members (not merely the teacher) in making the classroom a more real situation wherein students, according to their maturity and ability to learn, will develop in themselves the motivation and the responsibility for their own learning activity. In such a setting, the teacher should be able to concentrate on teaching, and students should be able to concentrate on learning, which, after all, is what schooling is supposed to be all about.

Stemming from this theoretical approach, the following general objectives can be identified:

1. Improved interpersonal communication.
2. Sensitivity to the effects of member behavior in group settings.
3. Understanding of the dynamics of working groups.
4. Intellectual and emotional involvement in the learning process.

Learnings take place on both personal and interpersonal levels:

Personal	Interpersonal
Understanding one's own feelings	Understanding feelings of others
Skill in communicating feelings	Skill in group task and maintenance behaviors
Self direction	
Self responsibility	Ability to diagnose communication problems
Intrinsic motivation	Full membership participation

SPECIFIC OBJECTIVES

A careful examination of the general objectives stated above reveals that they are written in terms of teaching; not in terms of teaching x or teaching y or teaching z, but in terms of just plain teaching. Put in another way, these objectives are concerned with the process of teaching rather than with its content. Such an emphasis does not deny the importance of content; rather, it seeks to focus on the process of teaching and learning the content, be it industrial arts, Latin, history, or some other phase of the curriculum.

As background to a consideration of methodology in the following chapters, it is necessary: (1) to define process, (2) to specify the behaviors that make up process, and (3) to suggest a way to make these behaviors apparent so that they can be learned and improved.

PROCESS IN TEACHING AND LEARNING

In any social situation, there are two levels on which communication takes place. The first and most familiar is the subject under discussion, or the *content level;* the second concerns the effects of member behavior on themselves and on the others, or the *process level.* When a teacher explains something on the chalkboard and encourages students to ask questions, and when a little girl does ask a question, and when the teacher brushes her aside by impatiently stating that this question has already been clearly answered, several communications have been made. On the content level, there has been explanation of the subject matter, a request for possible questions, a question, and an answer. On the process level, there has been a teacher denial of what he seemed to be asking for. Also, there has been an inhibiting of further student questions. Who wants to take the chance of being called stupid or of losing ground in the constant fight for high grades? Also, there has been a decrease in trust of the teacher; one had better take whatever he says in the future with a large grain of salt.

Of course, other kinds of messages could flow in the process level. Perhaps some or all of the students were as tired as the teacher of this girl's questions, which constantly seemed to prove that she hadn't been listening. Perhaps many messages were sent and received, but none of them were very clear, nor was response clear.

Clarity of reception and response on the content level cannot be assumed either, but it has become traditional to check this through class questions, student recitation, and written examinations. Most teachers have had the experience of being sure that students knew thoroughly what had been taught only to get a mess of misinformation handed back on a pen-and-paper test. Though such an experience may be disappointing, it is helpful because the teacher then knows that reteaching must be done and what areas must be stressed.

Tradition supports exploring and clarifying the content level of classroom communication, and teachers are constantly at work attempting to improve methods of presenting, discussing, and evaluating on this level. Yet the process level, which can develop feelings and attitudes to block or to enhance learning remains largely unexplored in many classrooms.

For many teachers, a discussion of student feelings (process level) to say nothing of their own seems a touchy subject, and the safest way to deal with feelings appears to be to pretend they do not exist—that the only thing going on in the classroom is the transmission of subject matter (content level). Despite the most elaborate pretense, however, other things *are* going on, and they come out in terms of inattention, withdrawal, refusal to do any more than the minimum requirements, and in overt "discipline problems." When these reactions become disruptive, the teacher is often forced to take action, but this action comes quite late, is usually punitive in nature, and may not be clearly seen in relation to its cause. A simple family illustration of this communications breakdown is seen in the father who, upon returning home at six in the evening, is asked to punish a young child who misbehaved at ten in the morning.

The teacher who screams at a misbehaving student, sends youngsters out of the room for deviant actions, changes seats, or keeps a whole class in after school is often treating symptoms instead of causes. In point of fact, he may not even be treating the symptoms, but merely requesting that students keep them to themselves and cooperate in the game of "Let's pretend that none of us are ever affected emotionally by anything that goes on in this class." But many students just cannot play this game all the time, and so devices have been developed including

banishment from the classroom; a trip to the principal, or the
dean of students, or the guidance office; a session or sessions in
a detention hall after school; or expulsion from school for a few
days (after which the student returns to begin the process all
over again). Little wonder that students drop out of school
physically or psychologically.

No real magic has been developed to combat behavior
problems—or processes that often make communication difficult—but our traditional wisdom does seem to support the
notion that running away from or attempting to ignore difficult
situations is of little help.

But recognizing them and dealing with them is not easy.
Mere teacher determination to explore the process level of
communication in a class will not assure instant success. What
is needed in addition is the incorporation in the teacher's attitude structure of a belief that the exploration of the process
level is important in a teaching-learning situation and a subsequent teacher mastery of techniques for such exploration. Presentation of techniques is the job of this book; teacher attitude
will come only from trial and, perhaps, some error.

CONTENT AND PROCESS BEHAVIORS

Benne and Sheats and others[7] have identified *behaviors,*
functions, or *roles,* which describe things that people do in aggregates or groups in order to get the job done (or, sometimes,
in order to *prevent* the job getting done). To avoid confusion
over these three terms, which are sometimes used synony-
mously, they may be defined as follows:

Behaviors   actions of individual group members expressed
            in verbal and/or non-verbal terms

Functions   behaviors directed purposefully toward build-
            ing the group and toward helping it accomplish
            its task.

[7]Benne, Kenneth D. and Paul Sheats, "Functional Roles of Group Members," *Journal of Social Issues*, 4, 2:41–49, 1948. See also Gibb, John R. and
Lorraine M. Gibb, eds., "Spotlight on Member Roles," *Adult Leadership*, I,
8:2–23, January, 1953.

(e.g., harmonizing is a behavior which can be called a function since it implies intent to affect the building of the group.)

Roles   characteristic playing of certain sets of functions by group members.

For the purposes of this discussion, the term *functions*, as defined above, will be used.

Task Functions

With the development over the years of what might be called the American "Cult of Efficiency,"[8] there is great individual anxiety in aggregates over the possibility of wasting time. Thus, a typical committee called for the purpose of accomplishing a certain task rarely takes time to get to know each other or to deal with its process level in any way. It is much too intent on making decisions and taking quick action. In getting the work done, one or more of the members must contribute behaviors that can be termed *task functions*. Some of these are:

Initiating: stating or defining the group task, stating goals, suggesting action, proposing plans, supplying ideas for the accomplishment of the task, making suggestions for the use of resources.

Supplying Information: giving facts, providing data relevant to concerns of group.

Giving Opinion: stating feelings as to the workability of plans, giving ideas as to whether they may or may not be accepted.

Requesting Information: Identifying areas where facts and concepts are needed, asking for suggestions and ideas.

Providing Information: Listing possible resource people or materials, bringing in solutions developed in other places, using one's own background and expertise.

Requesting Opinion: calling for member expression of feeling about procedures or ideas, asking for acceptance or rejection of objectives or proposals.

[8]For a treatment of researches that moved out of the "Efficiency Expert" approach in industry and into a human relations framework to increase worker output see Roethlisberger, F. J. and W. J. Dickson. *Management and the Worker.* Cambridge, Mass.: Harvard University Press, 1939.

Clarifying: restating ideas of others in one's own terms, questioning proposals, interpreting.

Elaborating: building on ideas of others, restating one's own ideas in more complex form.

Summarizing: restating main ideas proposed at any point, combining ideas of others in single form.

Consensus Testing: stating conclusion or decision and asking for group commitment, calling for vote or general agreement.

Evaluating: reminding group of deadlines, keeping minutes.

Orienting: keeping discussion relevant and on track.

Maintenance Functions

While the supplying of task functions by the leader and/or members should lead to effective task accomplishment, it does not always succeed, and quite often the work of the members is slow and inefficient. Such blocks to progress and member satisfaction are common in an aggregate where the social needs of members are ignored. What seems needed are behaviors that act to build more of a group feeling—an intragroup respect and rapport. Such group building maintenance functions are:

Recognizing: use of names in group discussion, giving of credit for good ideas or actions.

Accepting: expressions of friendliness and warmth, smiling and head nodding, indicating that one's absence is regretted and that one's presence is noted and welcome.

Harmonizing: helping others to understand the basis of their disagreements, reconciling conflicts, helping members to see the other fellow's point.

Compromising: helping others to combine their ideas into a mutually satisfactory proposal, giving ground on one's position in favor of a more generally acceptable statement, giving consent or commitment to an experimental tryout of a not yet personally acceptable idea.

Norm Testing: trying out procedures seemingly agreed upon by the group to find out if they are really acceptable.

Communication Facilitating: helping others to participate, making process-level comments, exploring personal feelings, voicing perceptions of the group feeling.

Individual Roles

A collection of people can become an effective group if they provide behaviors that meet both work and emotional needs of the members. The provided behaviors, in the form of task and maintenance functions, can result in sharing of leadership and responsibility by each individual member. Or the aggregate can behave in such a way as to remain an aggregate from session to session. When this happens, the submerged and unmet needs of members often lead to the playing of individual roles such as those detailed on page 61.

It is easy enough to scorn these individual roles and to condemn those who play them. What is more difficult, but more helpful, is to raise questions about the *process* of a group, which makes such role playing necessary for some individuals.

If these role descriptions are realistic, if such behaviors *do* occur in aggregates or groups—they certainly can prevent the accomplishment of any task such as learning. The teacher can use the big stick of institutional authority to suppress these symptoms of group malfunction, *or he can use them as potential learning experiences.* More and more evidence is piling up in American schools that suppression is not working. Perhaps teachers ought to try some alternative approaches.

To deal constructively with the malfunction caused by individual roles, the group needs to create an atmosphere in which it can look searchingly at its process level the way it now looks at its content level. Always remembering that the player of the individual role is a member of the group, group members need to project more acceptance and understanding of its members. By playing an individual role, the person so behaving is proclaiming his needs without stating them in words. The sad part about the communication is that his behavior, in an uncaring aggregate, usually succeeds in doing just the opposite of what he wants. What can be done?

As the material on page 61 suggests, each of these members playing individual roles have potential value for the group. If the group can respond to them in a helpful, non-punitive way, they may be able to meet their individual needs without resort-

Individual Role	Behavior	Need	Potential Value
Dictator	dominates, does not listen, exerts strong pressure using fast talk, loud voice, sarcasm	to be seen as group leader	takes position. establishes direction.
Prize Fighter	argues, criticizes, picks fights, encourages others to fight.	to get the action started	keeps things lively, provokes group action
Playboy	treats all discussion as source of hilarity, makes inappropriate jokes, mocks serious proposals	to demonstrate humor and superiority	relieves tension, makes people laugh.
Apple Shiner	supports everything teacher says, sides with dictators, never makes waves	to be accepted, particularly by dominant group figures	provider of support and encouragement as well as recognition
Point Picker	takes issue with everything anyone says, never really agrees or gives consent to a group decision	to be seen as thoughtful intellectual	Devil's advocate. Loyal opposition, calls for careful examination of all sides of question
Martian Observer	sits silently, answers direct questions with terse comments and returns to silence	to avoid being revealed as inadequate	provides the group with a question as to the effects of its process, can make the group proud and close by finally participating
Marble Taker	withdraws into silence after ideas have been challenged or ignored	to be appreciated by others	also challenges the aggregate to become more sensitive as a group

ing to these roles which block the group in its operation. On their parts, the individuals must make some effort to learn more effective behavior.

The Dictator needs to learn that his forceful leadership will be more acceptable if he stops pushing it down people's throats, and that the resistance of others is not based on rejection of his ideas but rather on his methods. The Prize Fighter needs to learn that action is good, but that purposeless conflict is just plain annoying. He might help himself by thinking through his purposes and getting action started in more appropriate ways. The Playboy needs to be more selective in his efforts at joking and to see more clearly the difference between humor and silliness. The Apple Shiner and the Point Picker need to use their abilities in more constructive ways and develop the self-confidence to try other necessary group functions when they are needed. The Martian Observer and the Marble Taker need group acceptance and support very badly, but they also need to reward those who do try to help by moving, even slightly, away from their rigid positions of withdrawal.

PROCESS AND THE TOTAL GROUP

All of the foregoing is really a restatement in behavioral terms of questions teachers have asked themselves for generations. How do I get Johnny involved in the class? How do I prevent Sam from bullying his classmates without making him resentful or withdrawn? How do I tell Mary that she doesn't have to lick my boots to get my approval? What do I do for Joan, who is getting to be the most disliked girl in the class? Probably, the only really different note struck in this book is the notion that such problems are properly those of the total group and not just the teacher's alone. If the teacher can teach the class how to deal with its process as well as its content, he may be holding the key to a rich educational experience that will not only increase learning potential but expand its base. He might begin by asking himself what is the real value of learning subject matter if one does not also increase one's ability to be a satisfied, effective human being.

4

Interaction
Exercises

IN THE PRECEDING chapter, the notion of a process level of communication was developed, and it was suggested that groups
explore this level just as most now explore the content level.
Further, it was suggested that the group as a whole do this
rather than leaving the entire job to the teacher.

To accomplish such a task, group members must first become aware of the behaviors that make up the process level,
and then they must develop skills of data-gathering and analysis. For the development of such awareness and skill, the exercises in this chapter may be used as beginnings for the
teacher.

ROLE PLAYING

In the usual sense of the term, role playing is similar in
nature to stage acting. Participants are given roles—and perhaps
specific instructions as to how to play them—and they act out a
situation for the purpose of increasing their own insight into
how such people might feel in this situation, or for the purpose
of providing data for an observing group, or for both these purposes. The two exercises that follow may be used with role
instructions or by allowing participants to play themselves. It is
important to note that they are all designed to get at specific
objectives. They should be used within the context of the
regular classroom situation.

Triple Group Exercise

This activity may be used from the beginning of the first class session. Theory is presented *after* the experience so that the experience itself creates a readiness to understand the theory. Objectives may be stated as follows: As a result of the exercise: (1) students will begin to understand the forces that block communication in classroom groups, (2) individuals will begin to express themselves more freely in the class, (3) the class, including the teacher, will begin to become closer as a group, and (4) students will develop a readiness to participate actively in course planning, course discussions, and evaluation of their learning.

The procedure is used for class groups numbering eighteen to thirty-six students. Steps in conducting the exercise are as follows:

1. Teacher begins by telling class that since they will be spending a semester (or a year) together it would be helpful at the outset to learn something about how people work in groups. In order to begin this learning, some members of the class will do a group-work exercise while the others will observe. In this way, three things can be accomplished: (1) improvement of group work skills, (2) development of effective techniques for observation of groups at work, and (3) increased knowledge about each other and, perhaps, a more spontaneous and open atmosphere for classroom discussion.

2. Following this introduction, the teacher divides the class into three equal groups, designating them as groups A, B, and C. (Boys and girls may be segregated, evenly distributed, or randomly assigned in these groups.)

3. Arrange chairs in three concentric circles.

4. Pair off members of Groups A and B so that each student in Group A has a partner in Group B.

5. Group A (INTERACTING) sits in the center circle and each member places a name tag in front of him.

6. Group B (COACHING) sits in the second circle in such a way that each member can see the face of his partner in Group A.

7. Group C (OBSERVING) sits in the outside circle in random order.

8. Teacher distributes instruction sheets (see pp. 68–70) to each group, giving a few minutes for reading.

9. Teacher explains that Group C will be involved in general observation of Group A and that Group B will observe specific individuals in Group A. Group A will function for twenty minutes and then break into helping pairs with observer-partners from Group B. There will be ten minutes for these helping pairs during which time the teacher will chat with Group C concerning their observation of Group A as a whole.

10. When the three groups have been seated in concentric circles, the teacher reads aloud the instructions for the interacting group so that all members of the class know the task.

11. Teacher says, "I think we can begin now," and sits down. (Teacher may sit with Group A or elsewhere in the room. He may wish to take his own notes as to who participates, who leads, who helps the group, and who hinders it. Teacher's role is that of *silent observer*. Initially, this will be difficult for the teacher *and* for Group A because it departs from the usual expectation of *teacher talk–student listen*. The discovery by both the teacher and the class members that significant, effective things can go on without continual teacher domination is one of the most important parts of the exercise.

12. After initial self-consciousness, members begin to talk.

13. In twenty minutes, even though the group has not finished its task, teacher calls "Time. You will have ten minutes to confer with your observer coaches. You will want to know how they have seen you, and they will want to know if they have been clear and helpful. Group C will meet with me. You have ten minutes, and then we will return to the interacting group."

14. Helping pairs form in different parts of the room and teacher meets with Group C off to one side or in the hall if there is not enough space. Teacher asks Group C, "What did you observe?" and group members contribute their ideas. Teacher may also make *his* comments, being careful to encourage objectivity. The purpose is *not* to place blame of any sort on dominating or silent group members, but to look at results of their behavior on the group's activities.

15. After ten minutes, teacher brings Group A together again and the interaction plus observation resumes.

16. Five minutes before close of session, teacher again calls time, and each student writes his reactions to the experience. (Time allotment is five minutes for introductions, twenty minutes for interacting group, ten minutes for helping pairs, ten minutes for reconvened group, and five minutes for written reactions. This is a total of fifty minutes.)

17. At the beginning of the second session, the teacher may wish to comment on some of the written reactions. Then Group B becomes the interacting group in the center, Group C moves in to become the observer-coach group, and Group A moves to the outer circle to be general observers. The process above is repeated.

18. In the third session, Group C is the center interacting, Group A becomes the observer-coach group, and Group B moves to the outer circle as general observers. This gives each group a chance to experience all three positions.

19. In the fourth session, the class as a whole should have time to discuss the experience and share their individual feelings about it. At this time, the teacher can, if he wishes, take advantage of the open communication to explore student feelings about the course and how they would like to proceed.

20. At the fifth session, the class should have a readiness to engage in planning activities. This might be pupil-teacher planning, or it might be the teacher's explanation of how he has planned the course.

In five sessions of the course (five fifty-minute periods) the ice has been broken, students have heard the sound of their own voices, a level of trust and openness has begun, which can have great effect on the amount and level of student contributions to his class, and everyone has a sense of the direction in which the learnings will proceed.

To avoid the complete suspension of subject-centered activities during these opening sessions, mimeographed sheets or textbook assignments may be given by the teacher to be taken up in class following the sessions devoted to the exercise.

Though there will be initial confusion in the carrying out of the exercise, students will quickly adjust to it. Aside from the obvious benefit to the communications pattern of the class, the very novelty of the approach carries its own motivation.

Any encounter between human beings should occur only

after certain precautions are observed. (This, of course, would include any traditional classroom activities.) Two considerations occur in this exercise. First, the helping pair coaching aspect should be considered. Each person in the coaching group should attempt to say things that are specific and helping when conferring with a member of the interacting group. It is difficult enough to be part of a group operating in a "fishbowl" environment without being criticized harshly by one's observer. It should be emphasized that the observer is learning how to be *helpful*. He needs to put his comments in such a way that the receiver can accept them and take them in the spirit given.

Second, the teacher must be aware of the potential being opened. If he does *not* want open communication, if he is most comfortable in the dictator role in his classroom, then perhaps he does not need such an exercise. If he does want open communication, then he must be aware of the fact that such an exercise is *only the beginning*. Full advantage will occur only if this opening is followed by free expression and evaluation throughout the course. In almost all cases, years of teacher domination will have preceded this exercise, and student self-direction and self-responsibility will not happen magically in a short time. If and when such conditions do develop, both teacher and students have an unusual and enriching experience.

The three sheets following, titled Interacting Group, Observer-Coach Guide, and General Observation, are given to the students at the beginning of each session (see step #8). They serve a dual purpose. First, they instruct students in what is to begin, and second, they allow for written reactions that are helpful for both teachers and students. The wording may be modified according to student maturity and reading level.

INTERACTING GROUP INSTRUCTIONS

As a member of the interacting group, you have the rather rare opportunity to write the text and then read it. The text will be the sum of interactions of your group, and your reading will be your analysis of the types of behaviors which helped and of those which hindered the formation of a group by the strangers who sat down together.

You and your group have the task of finding a task to accomplish. There are really no right and wrong ideas so yours are as good as anyone else's. The only outside requirement is that you go about the job in such a way that this collection of individuals begins to become a cohesive group.

Your name _____.

Your reactions to the experience in general:

Figure 7.

OBSERVER COACH GUIDE INSTRUCTIONS

Your Name ———————. Observer's Name ———————.

You will focus on a single member of the interacting group so that you can mirror his behavior to him. Your comments will be in the form of, "As I saw you, you . . . ." Your behavior in the helping pair will be directed to helping *him* to think through his own behavior in the group.

Attempt, below, to describe your observee's behavior in the group. Was he quiet, domineering, helpful to others? Did he support and/or clarify the contributions of others? Did he help the group to formulate its goals?

Attempt, below, to report, as you saw it, the effects of your observee's behavior on the other members of the group. Did they react, and if so what were reactions?

Figure 8.

GENERAL OBSERVER INSTRUCTIONS

Your Name _____. Group No. _____.

You will focus on the interaction pattern of the whole group rather than on the behavior of a specific participant. Following the interaction session, you will have opportunity to compare your findings with those of others in *your* group.

You will want to note who speaks most and least, who the leaders of the group appear to be, what behaviors seem to produce group action and satisfaction, what behaviors seem to block the group in getting at its task, and whether the group acts as an *entire* group, as a collection of sub-groups, or as an assortment of individuals.

Make your notes below. Specific quotes of significant speeches are helpful.

Figure 9.

Diagnostic Skill Session

While an activity such as the triple group exercise can be used to build a readiness for interaction in the classroom, specific training in group awareness and skills needs a more specific approach. Since student working committees are often formed in the classroom, and since they are rarely helped to diagnose their problems, committee work might be a good subject for a group exercise.

One hypothetical setting for such an exercise might be a tenth-grade mathematics class with twenty-eight students. (Twenty-eight is used for the purposes of illustration. Adjustments can be made for more or for less students.)

Three weeks ago, this class carried out a unit using student committees, which were assigned the task of developing a way to clearly present a mathematical concept to the rest of the class. The teacher's purpose here was to motivate student inquiry into the work of the course, reasoning that students would have to apply themselves diligently to the learning in order to be able to explain the processes to others. His role was to be available as a resource to each committee as it worked. A secondary goal was student learning in terms of working with others and in verbalizing one's learning.

While worthwhile mathematical learning took place, the committee work was somewhat slow and fumbling at the beginning. Students had mixed feelings about their ability to work well together, though most saw the activity as an interesting one.

The teacher sensed that the students who contributed least to the committee work were the same students who withheld participation in general class. He realized that group work was difficult because students had never been taught to evaluate and improve their operations. Since the use of committees, while not an unqualified success, had improved the number and the depth of student questions, he felt that it should be tried again. This time, however, he decided to include two sessions of diagnostic skill training.

To begin with, he (1) wrote a situation that had direct

meaning for his class, (2) developed role instructions for the role players, (3) wrote guidelines for observers, and (4) jotted down a few discussion questions. They looked like this:

Situation Statement

You are a classroom committee formed to plan the presentation of a mathematical concept to the rest of the class. The teacher has assigned you the idea that in a right triangle the sum of the squares of the sides are equal to the square of the hypotenuse.

This is your first meeting as a group. You will have about twenty minutes to make a tentative decision as to how you will handle the assignment and who will do what.

Role Player Instructions

(Note: Since the number of students in this hypothetical class is twenty-eight, two groups of fourteen can be formed, and half of each group will be role players while the other half will observe. This means that seven separate roles are needed. Role instructions should be designed so that problems common to such groups will occur. The role playing is really a way of illustrating problems so that they may be analyzed and discussed. Name of role players should be different from any names in the class.)

JOHN: You are used to leading groups, and you are a bit impatient with the time other students take to make decisions. You have the procedure all planned out, and you can save time by just telling the group about it and telling the other members what to do. If anyone has a different idea or calls for a chairman, you should express a great deal of impatience. Why waste time? If the group doesn't accept your idea, it will just talk and get nowhere. Push for the acceptance of your idea, and withdraw into silence if you are blocked. You'll show them!

HOWARD: You resent John because he always pushes his ideas on the group and will not listen to anyone else. You don't mind hearing his ideas, but you want to see everyone's ideas expressed so that the group can make a choice. If John starts off by pushing people around, you will move to block him by asking that everyone contribute an idea. Don't let him be the boss. Try to include everyone.

MARY: You like Howard and will move to support any ideas he presents. Say things like, "Howard's idea makes a lot of sense. Why don't we try it?" If you make a really good impression on Howard, maybe he will invite you to the dance.

ROSE: You are as impatient as John to get something done, but you agree with Howard that more people ought to be heard. You wish they would stop fighting because it makes it impossible for the group to get anywhere. Let them go at it for awhile and then say something like, "We're not getting anywhere. I wish we could just make a decision." If Mary says anything, ask her what her suggestion is. If anyone suggests having a chairman, throw up your hands and say, "We're wasting time. We don't need a chairman. We need to get to work.

JANE: You are not sure just what to do, and you are afraid to say the wrong thing. Therefore, you remain silent unless someone asks you a direct question. If someone does, try to indicate that you agree with everyone, but do not say very much. If anyone complains about your silence, tell him that it is your business and to leave you alone.

PETER: You want the committee to work. While you know that Howard and John will probably fight, you feel that you can make the peace. When people begin to argue, you point out that they both have good ideas and that some compromise

should be worked out. Another important contribution you make is that of summarizing. After
everyone has had a chance to speak, you will list
all the points they have made and ask, "Have I
left anything out?"

FRANK: You want to be the leader of the group, and you
see the appointment of a chairman as the way to
do it. Therefore, you will push for the election
of a chairman, mentioning that you yourself have
been a chairman of a group before. Agree that
everyone has a good idea, but that the whole discussion will be a mess unless there is a chairman
to keep order. If John, who is usually talkative,
grows silent, you will point out that with John
and Jane not saying anything, the group can't
really function.

The teacher should instruct role players to read role instructions over until they get all the ideas clear. They should
play the roles to the hilt, but should avoid overplaying them.
If the players do not seem to be playing the roles correctly, the
teacher may stop the proceedings and have them reread the
instructions.

Observer Guidelines

In each subgroup of fourteen there will be seven role
players and seven observers. When the role play ends, each
observer will report his observations of the player to whom
he was assigned. To help him with this task, the teacher will
prepare a sheet that will suggest what it is he is looking for
and on which he can make notes. Such a sheet is illustrated
in Figure 10.

Guide for Observers

As an observer, your task is to select a particular role player to observe, sit so that you face him or her, note your observations on this sheet, and be prepared to report your findings at the end of the role playing. (It is helpful if you take down actual words used.)

1. Comment on the concerns of your observee. Was he or she thinking of others in the group or merely focussed on self?

2. Describe his or her actions. What effect did they seem to have on the others? Helpful? Hindering?

Figure 10

General Observation Instructions

Your task is to observe the group as a whole in order to determine what the leadership situation is, whether everyone is participating, and what is helping or blocking the group.

1. Is the leadership in the hands of one or two people or is it shared by the group?

2. Who speaks to whom? Does everyone participate?

3. What is the atmosphere in the group? Tense? Comfortable? Silly?

Figure 11

The teacher may wish to have one or two students make general observations of the group. This is particularly necessary if there are more than twenty-eight students. When this is the case, he may use the instructions in Figure 11.

Following the role playing and the reports by the observers, the teacher will want to lead a discussion and analysis of what has occurred. In order to channel the contributions of the students, he may wish to prepare a set of questions. Figure 12 illustrates.

Having developed these materials, the teacher is ready to proceed with the exercise. This will be a Monday through Friday, or five-session affair. Orientation will take one session, role playing two sessions, and group planning will take two sessions. By the following Monday the groups should be ready to report.

Discussion Questions

The exercise in which you have just participated raises certain questions about how groups function. Your responses in writing to the following questions will be helpful in our discussion. (Use back of sheet if necessary.)

1. How do the hidden feelings of members affect the work of a committee?

2. How can a group involve *all* its members?

3. How could the functioning of the role-playing group have been improved?

Figure 12

To begin, the class is divided into four committees of equal size: A, B, C, and D. For the two days of the role playing, groups A and B will be together and groups C and D will be joined. For Thursday and Friday, each group will operate as a separate committee. The procedure is as follows:

Five Day Exercise

1. FIRST SESSION: (*Monday*). Teacher has chosen a mathematical concept to be taught to his class. He has analyzed it into four operations that have to be understood to grasp the main concept. He has prepared written assignments for each operation keyed to the text plus supplemental readings in the library.

2. Teacher brings to class seven copies of each of the four operation assignments, twenty-eight sheets in all, one for each student.

3. At the beginning of the class, he creates four committees of seven students each (A–B–C–D), and hands out the written assignments. While they read them, he answers questions and clarifies what is to be done.

4. Each student, as an individual, is to do the assignment at home, using the library as necessary. Assignments are to be completed by Thursday.

5. After twenty minutes clarifying the assignment, the teacher reminds the class of their decision to try committee work again and announces that the next two days in class will be spent in what should be an interesting activity. It will consist of half the class working out a typical committee meeting while the rest observe and comment.

6. The teacher then informs the class that two of the committees (A and B) will form one group for the exercise and that the other two (D and C) will form a second group. Each group will then number fourteen.

7. In order to save time during the next session, the class will run through the exercise now.

8. Group A–B will meet at one end of the room while group C–D meets at the other. Their first task is to form seven pairs in each group.

9. One of each pair will be a role player; the other member of the pair will be his observer.

10. Teacher hands out one written role to each role player. (This means that the teacher needs to have two copies of each role.)

11. Role players are instructed: (1) not to let the others read the role; (2) to read the roles carefully; (3) to imagine how they would play these roles; and (4) to reread the roles to see if they have missed anything.

10. While the role players study their roles, the teacher gives out observer sheets to the remainder of the students. He explains that the students are to observe the process rather than the content of the role players' interactions.

11. Teacher then calls both groups together and explains that the role players will sit in an inner circle with their observers facing them. The seating would be as follows:

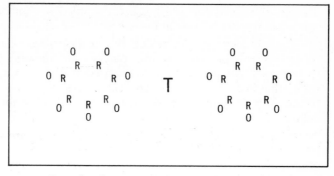

R—role players; O—observers; T—teacher

12. Teacher has each group seat themselves in the concentric circles so that they will know how to do it. They will take these seats immediately upon entering the class at the next session.

13. He then collects the role-playing instructions and the observer guide sheets so that they can be handed out at the beginning of the next session.

14. SECOND SESSION: (*Tuesday*). Students enter and seat themselves in the two sets of concentric circles.

15. Teacher hands out sheets. In addition, he hands out tags with role names written large with magic marker on filing cards or oak tag. This will focus observers on the roles rather than on the actual students.

16. Teacher directs role players to read through their instructions and checks to see whether each role player has an observer. (In case of absence, he will have to make changes.)

17. Teacher reads the situation to both groups and reads it again. He answers clarifying questions and then directs role players to begin.

18. Role players begin their interaction, and the teacher keeps time. After about twenty minutes he breaks in (role players do not have to have finished) and directs observers to report their observations. Directly following each oral report, the role player reads his written instructions so that group can see how close the observer came.

19. Following this, the teacher leads a full class discussion on the question sheets, which are handed out at this time. There will be time only for a brief discussion, but the stu-

dents will take the sheets home to be filled out and returned at the next session of the class.

20. Teacher announces that during the next session today's observers will become the role players and today's role players will become observers. The new role players will drop the instructions and play themselves in the same situation to see whether they can improve the group interaction.

21. THIRD SESSION: (*Wednesday*). The two groups reconvene with reversed roles. The teacher again reads the situation and tells the groups to begin. (Fresh observer sheets are needed for this session.)

22. Teacher allows groups to run about twenty minutes or until they reach a decision. Then he stops them.

23. This time, each group will form a fourteen-member circle to discuss their observations and feelings for ten minutes.

24. For the remainder of the period, the entire class will discuss the exercise in terms of the homework questions and the discussions they have just finished.

25. At the end of the session, the teacher announces that the exercise is over and that the committees will begin their work tomorrow, having a chance to put new understandings and learnings to the test in an actual situation.

26. FOURTH SESSION: (*Thursday*). The four committees meet to begin their planning. They will spend the last ten minutes of the period discussing their process.

27. FIFTH SESSION: (*Friday*). Groups will finish their planning, decide on which days they will report to the class, and again check their process during the last ten minutes.

This exercise should provide the class with an interesting experience and should measurably improve each group's performance. (See Chapter five for evaluation procedures.)

In addition to the specific committee work, the awareness of the process level of communication can have far-reaching effects on participation in the class if the exercise is followed up. Such followup might include setting aside fifteen minutes each week to ask, "How are we doing?" In these sessions, the teacher should also participate, talking about how he feels toward the class. Does he feel that students are participating? Are they taking any responsibility for their own learning? Are they raising any really thoughtful questions about the subject matter?

Are they supplying maintenance functions in class discussion in order to help their fellow classmates feel more free to participate?

Since the enhancement of communication flow and the development of an uninhibited atmosphere for learning needs to be nurtured through teacher and student interactions, two points should be underlined. First, participation can be a much more meaningful activity than it is in many classrooms. Participation is not mere talk or response to a recitation method where the teacher asks questions and individual students answer with little awareness of each other. It is interesting to see a student whose raised hand has been recognized by the teacher begin to answer the question. If he becomes unsure of his response or falters at any moment, ten other hands shoot up instantly with no discernible consideration for his feelings.

At the same time, many hands are *not* raised, and one wonders what is going on in the owners' minds. The end result is that students do not really explore ideas or help each other to understand the subject matter more fully. Yet, with many hands in the air, many teachers are pleased at the "participation" in the class. What is suggested in the notion of interaction analysis is that this student eagerness is only a first step and needs much further development.

The second point to be underlined is that the exercises in this book are meant as beginnings. After a month or two of being together, awareness and skills in both content and process levels ought to become internalized so that there is less need for crutches. But the crutches *are* necessary in the beginning if teacher and students are to break through the overformality that makes the classroom more a game than a vital and meaningful part of living.

BUILDING THE GROUP

In order to move toward group status, any aggregate of people must find a mutually satisfactory way of meeting two kinds of needs. They must feel a sense of progress toward goals (*task functions*), and they must develop a supportive atmosphere (*maintenance functions*). Needs for progress begin to be met when members internalize goals—when they begin to relate them to their own personal framework of understanding, put them in their own language, and see them as personally valuable. This is best done by having members participate in the formulation of goals.

Needs for a supportive atmosphere begin to be met when members recognize the contributions of others, call them by name, and indicate that they have heard what others have said. Without such a supportive atmosphere, only a few strong members speak out, and even they tend to seek a dependency relationship with the appointed leader (in this case, the teacher).

Goal progress rests on internalization, and atmosphere progress rests on interpersonal knowledge and respect. This latter condition is commonly called "getting to know each other."

Work on both these areas should begin early in the life span of any classroom group, and since progress is difficult, this work should be reinforced as the year unfolds. Many avenues toward progress exist, and the inventive teacher will undoubtedly develop his own methods. One approach that seems workable on many age levels is the following:

Background Sharing Exercise

SITUATION: This is a class in (*fill in grade level and subject*). It is the first week of the school year. Students know some of their fellows, but not all. Each has had some experiences in the subject during the preceding year(s) and/or expectations concerning this year's work. Each, also, has a wealth of hobbies, interests, experiences, and aspirations, which have developed during the years in which he has lived. In addition, he has probably come to believe that most of this background is not relevant to normal classroom behavior. He probably sees communication with his peers in the classroom mostly in terms of misbehavior, and feels quite inadequate in setting his own goals for learning. After all, that is the teacher's job.

INTENT: The teacher realizes the norms of dependency and inter-student competition that have been developed by many teachers. He also accepts his own position as subject matter expert. There certainly *are* valid reasons why *he* is the teacher and *they* are the students. However, he feels that student internalization of learning goals plus the creation of a mutually supportive atmosphere are vital ingredients in effective teaching and learning. His initial intent is to aid his class in re-evaluating and changing the classroom norms they have come to expect. Feeling that a lecture on this subject would be less effective than a shared experience, he structures the first few sessions of the class in such a way that students are active from the beginning.

GENERAL
CONDITIONS:

1. Norm changing is a delicate and difficult process. Teacher cannot expect immediate success. Patience and faith are needed.

2. Natural fears of "wasting time" and "failing to cover the ground" will occur to both teacher and students, since they are not accustomed to this new way of learning. Justification must come from the fact that the teacher *is* dealing directly with the subject matter, that he is involved in teaching study skills, and that he is motivating the class.

3. It is important that the teacher explain the exercise and why he thinks it is important. He should enlist his students' feeling of adventure. A feeling of "Let's explore together" is a vital prerequisite.

4. As the exercise proceeds, the students will probably be wondering whether the teacher is really sincere. Does he really want them to get to know each other? Does he really value what *they* think about the course? After all, they've been fooled before.

5. Students will need help in learning how to go about expressing their ideas and developing them into proposals for learning. (Even the teacher could use sharpening of his own skills in this area.)

Goals: Teacher purposes for this exercise may be expressed as follows: As a result of this experience, students will:

1. know each other's names,
2. know something about each other in terms of hobbies, interests, and ambitions,

3. feel freer to speak out in class,
4. tend more to support each other,
5. review previous learnings in this subject,
6. develop and describe future learnings,
7. define and list resources in terms of films, printed materials, the community, field trip opportunities, and human resources such as the librarian,
8. suggest ways of learning this subject,
9. suggest ways in which the specialized knowledge of the teacher can best be used.

Procedures

1. SESSION ONE: Teacher asks class whether all students know each other. If there are some who do not, the teacher suggests that since they will spend a school year together, it would probably help to get acquainted. Next, he asks what they know about the subject and what they expect to learn this year.
2. (Since a beginning class is an aggregate, and since the question of expectations is a difficult one, it may be expected that a few students will struggle with it while the rest remain silent.)
3. After five minutes discussion, the teacher says that he has a number of ideas himself, but that he would like to know what they think first. He realizes that this is not an easy assignment, and would they like to try an experiment.
4. The student response will probably be a tentative yes subject to hearing more about the teacher's idea.
5. Teacher explains that what he has in mind should help students to know each other better and develop their problem-solving abilities. Both of these will be important to the work of the class in future.
6. The exercise will consist of meeting in pairs for five minutes, combining pairs into quartets for five minutes, combining quartets into octets for ten minutes, and writing the results of octet discussions for five minutes.
7. Each subgrouping will have two tasks: (1) to share names, hobbies, and interests; (2) to determine two or three things that they especially want to learn in this course.
8. To begin the procedure, the teacher assigns each student a number in random fashion (e.g., in a class of 32 students, 1, 2, 3 . . . 32).

Organization of Sessions

SESSION ONE:

Orientation (Procedures 1–8)   15 minutes

Pairs meet

1	2	3	4	5	6	7	8
9	10	11	12	13	14	15	16
17	18	19	20	21	22	23	24
25	26	27	28	29	30	31	32

5 minutes

Quartets meet:

1	2	3	4	5	6	7	8
9	10	11	12	13	14	15	16
17	18	19	20	21	22	23	24
25	26	27	28	29	30	31	32

5 minutes

Octets meet:

1	2	3	4	5	6	7	8
9	10	11	12	13	14	15	16
17	18	19	20	21	22	23	24
25	26	27	28	29	30	31	32

10 minutes

Octets will appoint a secretary to record with ball point pen on ditto master those things students have said they want to learn.   5 minutes

SESSION TWO:

Teacher has run off copies of yesterday's lists so that each student receives four sheets—one from each octet.

For the first five minutes, each student reads through the lists and makes notes as further ideas occur to him.

Format for the second session begins with the same pairs as first session, but changes the membership of the quartets and octets so that more face-to-face relationships develop. The assignment is the same: #7 of page 84.

Individual student reading and notemaking.   5 minutes

Pairs meet:

1	2	9	10	17	18	25	26
3	4	11	12	19	20	27	28
5	6	13	14	21	22	29	30
7	8	15	16	23	24	31	32

5 minutes

Quartets:

1	2	9	10	17	18	25	26
3	4	11	12	19	20	27	28
5	6	13	14	21	22	29	30
7	8	15	16	23	24	31	32

5 minutes

Octets:

1	2	9	10	17	18	25	26
3	4	11	12	19	20	27	28
5	6	13	14	21	22	29	30
7	8	15	16	23	24	31	32

10 minutes

Writing of revisions and additions from each
octet on paper to be handed to teacher.   10 minutes

SESSION THREE:

Teacher reviews student writing from session two and
organizes items under main headings. Copies are duplicated
for students.

For the first five minutes, each student will read and make
notes and additions on his sheet as in session two.

For the remainder of the session, the teacher will plan with
the class what is to be taught first, how it can be handled in
terms of method, what resources are available and how they
can be used, and what method of evaluation will be best.

During this session, the teacher's most valuable contribution
can be suggestions in terms of methods. Lectures, demonstra-
tions, discussions, projects, panels, committees, use of textbook, written and visual materials, field trips, guest speakers
and the like may be suggested where they seem appropriate.
It may be helpful to invite resource people from the staff to
come in for half the period to help in the planning (e.g., librarian, audio-visual director, curriculum director, school
nurse or doctor, school psychologist).

At this session, ideas of what objectives will be set, what
teacher and students will do, when they will do what, and
how they will evaluate—all these should be listed on chalkboard.

The task of organizing these ideas into a flow chart for a
month's work (or whatever time period seems appropriate)

will not be accomplished during this period—it will have to wait for session four.

SESSION FOUR:

The exercise thus far should do much to make the group more cohesive, but full participation will take much more time. At this point, the subgroups have met to share ideas, but they have not had the more difficult task of decision-making.

During session four, therefore, their asignment is to map out the activities for the next two to three or four weeks based on the points of discussion in session three.

As they move from group to larger group, they will have to make decisions by choosing from alternative plans or combining and modifying proposals.

In session four, they will begin with octets, move to sixteens, and finish as the full class.

Teacher should remind them that the norm of introductions and use of each other's names still applies. Teacher should sit in on some of the groups and reinforce maintenance functions.

Teacher reviews ideas of session three and assigns groups the task of deciding what will be done, when, and by whom.   10 minutes

Octets:

1	2	11	12	21	22	31	32
7	8	13	14	19	20	25	26
3	4	29	30	9	10	23	24
5	6	27	28	15	16	17	18

10 minutes

Sixteens:

1	2	11	12	21	22	31	32
7	8	13	14	19	20	25	26
3	4	29	30	9	10	23	24
5	6	27	28	15	16	17	18

10 minutes

Total Class: Final decision as to what will be done, when, and by whom. One student may record decision on chalkboard, using a checkerboard grid to indicate sessions.   15 minutes

SESSION FIVE:

This session, under teacher direction, may be used to tie up any loose ends. At the close of the period, everyone should know what is going to happen during the next few weeks and what part they and the teacher will play.

An important item for this session is a discussion of how well students think they got to know each other, and how they feel about this.

Though it is unlikely that the students will do anything like a perfect job of planning, the exercise should be a giant step toward learning how to plan for learning. The teacher may wish to hand out and collect a short reaction sheet at the end of session four. These data can spark the discussion of "How did we do?" during session five.

LISTENING SKILL SESSION

Thus far, the exercises have involved interacting groups of various sizes. Tasks have ranged from getting to know each other to sharpening group awareness of the process level of communication. From time to time, however, the teacher and/or the students may identify specific skills that need to be developed. One such specific skill is listening.

The idea of developing skill in listening seems, at first glance, to be an absurd one. People spend a good deal of their waking moments listening. Why should they have to develop a skill they already have? Perhaps a skill exercise in this area is necessary because listening is too often taken for granted. Actually, most groups that begin to look at their process as well as their content identify listening as a skill that needs improving.

It takes only a little thought to verify this statement. How many times do we have the experience of not really understanding what is being said? How many times are our messages misunderstood or only partly understood? Are we sometimes so concerned with what *we* are planning to say that we only partially listen to the other person? And when the listening is imperfect, how do we find out about it? Do we ask to have it repeated? If we repeated, in our words, what another has said, would he recognize it as his message? Is the act of listening really as simple as we think it is?

As it is used in this book, the concept of interaction would suggest a mutual responsibility of speaker and hearer in the listening process. Rather than the term, listening, then, it might be more accurate to think in terms of skill in concentration and mutual clarification.

In the following skill session, listening is examined behaviorally as a vital factor in the improvement of group communication.

Procedure

1. Teacher distributes (or writes on chalkboard) three or four discussion topics that he has composed out of his knowledge of the interests and backgrounds of his students.
2. He then divides the class into groups of three students seated as far apart as space permits.
3. He explains that each group must select one of the discussion topics. Give two or three minutes for this.
4. The trios are to discuss the topic they have chosen. Discussion is unstructured except that each person who speaks (except the first, of course) must paraphrase what the last person has said before he himself speaks. This paraphrasing must be done to the satisfaction of the last speaker.
5. Teacher allows discussions to continue for fifteen to twenty minutes. He then stops them and has them discuss the exercise for a few minutes still in the trios.
6. The short discussion is followed by a general class discussion concerning the experience. The following questions may be used as guidelines:

How difficult was it to paraphrase?

Did the difficulty depend on the clarity of the speaker?

Did it depend on how long he spoke or how many ideas he tried to get across at a time?

Did you find that *your* listeners had trouble with your messages?

Do you usually listen this intently?

Is it sometimes hard to follow ideas in class?

How can we improve our communication?

NON-DIRECTIVE DISCUSSION LEADERSHIP

Teacher direction is an essential part of each of the exercises detailed above. In explaining and motivating the group work and in the short talks at the end, the teacher's understanding of group process and skill in discussion leadership is a vital ingredient. As such, it should be considered separately.

It has been noted in Chapter two that the common pattern of classroom interaction is from the teacher to John, back to the teacher, to Mary, back to the teacher, to Fred, back to the teacher, and so on. This pattern may be most appropriate when the class is engaged in asking specific questions of the teacher; for the purposes of a discussion, however, it is most inappropriate. Good discussion leadership acts to bring out maximum participation and to extend the communications pattern so that student speaks to student without having to plug into the teacher switchboard.

Because students have learned through their schooling years to see the teacher as a switchboard, and because so many teachers play this role, a change in pattern will come about only through a change in teacher behavior. Such change should move from directive, dominating, dependency creating leadership toward non-directive, member freeing leadership.[1] In performing such a function (or set of functions), the teacher should seek to move out of his usual bottleneck position in the discussion while at the same time acting to reinforce students' confidence in their own ability. Since they tend to have limited self-confidence, they may be expected to make it difficult, at least initially, for the teacher to move. When the teacher begins to change the ways in which he plays his role, he begins to make it necessary for students to change behaviors that they are used to. Yet such change *is* possible, and it need not be painful. The results of the change are well worth the trouble since

---

[1]Gordon, Thomas. *Group-Centered Leadership; A Way for Releasing the Creative Power of Groups.* Boston: Houghton Mifflin Co., 1955. While the whole book is extremely valuable, Chapter eight; "A Description of the Group-Centered Leader" is especially relevant. See Also Rogers, Carl R., *Client-Centered Therapy,* Chapter IX, "Student-Centered Teaching," Boston: Houghton Mifflin Co., 1965.

there are few feelings as good as that of feeling competent in self-direction. Such an aim is what all schools say they strive for; non-directive discussion leadership is merely a first step in that direction.

Before proceeding further, it might be well to define the term and specify teacher behavior.

Non-directive teaching might perhaps better be called non-manipulating or non-suffocating teaching. It consists of teacher behavior designed to cut through the dependency needs of students by refusing to do their thinking and structuring for them. This does not mean, in any sense, that direction of some sort is not necessary; rather, it means that the teacher sees his role as fostering self-direction on the part of the students. This is not an easy process in the beginning for either teacher or students because of the preponderance of traditional practice that puts the teacher in the driver's seat and tends to glue him there through his own expression of ego need to be the giver of all knowledge and through the students' acceptance of a comfortable passive role. Speaking of the preparation of teachers to change their highly directive roles, Sarason and his colleagues have said:

> . . . . in describing our experiences we emphasize not the amount of time, but what we consider to be a way of structuring the relationship between students and instructors, which is different from more conventional procedures. Briefly, and to recapitulate: The students were rarely *given* ideas of starting points; they had to subject their ideas, opinions, and suggestions to discussion; they were more or less forced to learn to give expression to and to depend upon *their* curiosity; they could express their puzzlements and ignorance without viewing them as signs of stupidity but as aids to productive learning; and they were enabled to see for themselves the complexity and selectivity of their own observational processes and their effects on action. To accomplish these things, it is far from sufficient to say to students: "Be curious. Use your own ideas. Do not be afraid to be wrong! etc." Unless students actually begin to respond in these ways and in so doing experience an awareness of a change in their thinking and perspective, verbal suggestions are not likely to be effective. It is essential to our approach to expect that students will and must struggle, because

learning to think independently and to utilize one's own intellectual resources is never easy, particularly when previous learning has been of the passive, dependent variety.[2]

If such a non-directive stance is important, it certainly should begin with the teacher in his own training. That such teacher behavior is *not* characteristic of today's teachers is borne out in the results of an increasing number of studies that document through stenographic reports, tape recordings, and kinescopes what *is* going on in American classrooms. Typical of such studies is Bellack's, which reports that:

Teachers dominate the verbal activities of the classrooms studied. The teacher-pupil ratio of activity in terms of lines spoken is approximately 3 to 1; in terms of moves, the ratio is about 3 to 2. Therefore, regardless of the unit considered, teachers are considerably more active than pupils in amount of verbal activity.[3]

Non-directiveness on the part of the teacher stems from his understanding of the effects of various styles of leader behavior. Teachers, traditionally, are concerned with promoting student participation in the class. They tend to mention the participation rate often and frequently base part of a student's grade on his overt involvement in class discussion. Yet, as Gordon points out;

The more dependent the group is upon its leader, the more his contribution will inhibit the participation of other members. The greater the status or prestige differential is between the leader and the members (as perceived by the members), the more likely the leader's contributions will inhibit participation of the members.[4]

In response to such data, the teacher who feels that increasing student self-direction leads to worthwhile learning experiences may wish to modify the role he now plays as discussion leader. If so, he will want to try out some new leader behaviors.

[2]Sarason, Seymour B., Kenneth Davidson, and Burton Blatt. *The Preparation of Teachers.* New York: John Wiley and Sons, Inc., 1962, pp. 90–91. Used by permission.

[3]Bellack, Arno A. *Theory and Research in Teaching.* New York: Bureau of Publications, Teachers College, Columbia University, 1963, p. 110.

[4]Gordon. *Group-Centered Leadership,* p. 250.

Such new behaviors emphasize restructuring the usual communication network, which makes him willingly or unwillingly a bottleneck that serves to block free student-to-student interaction. In seeking to accomplish this modification, he will realize that student behavior will also have to change and that this will not happen immediately. In effect, he is attempting to teach his students skills in interaction.

1. Teacher begins with the recognition that the traditional seating arrangement in rows was developed for efficiency in one-way transmission of information.

2. If he wishes to encourage students to speak to students, he will have to seat them in a circle or semi-circle.

3. Since knowledge of a subject is prerequisite to its discussion, the topic should be one that has been experienced by the students either directly or through instructional materials.

4. Some class discussions will center on subject matter, some on methodology, some on evaluation of what has been done.

5. Motivation will probably center on the degree of feeling that participants bring to the subject matter of a discussion. If few care one way or the other, no method or gimmick of some sort will be successful in involving the students.

6. The teacher may begin by stating (or restating) the problem, though as the group begins to mature, this role can be taken by a student.

7. As students begin to express feelings and opinions or to ask questions, it should be expected initially that these will be addressed to the teacher as judge, final arbiter, and fount of all really worthwhile knowledge and opinion.

8. It is the teacher's job at this junction to clarify and reflect what has been said, but avoiding a bottlenecking role even when students attempt to place him within it.

9. In the playing of a non-directive role, the teacher will:
   a. Listen and communicate to the class that he is aware of and interested in what is being said.
   b. Accept and respect students' ideas while helping them clarify their thoughts.
   c. Reflect ideas by rephrasing them to be sure that full meaning is communicated.

d. Reflect feelings by raising questions when he senses responses not being stated directly.
e. Help students to elaborate their own and others' ideas.
f. Connect ideas and builds concepts from what students are saying.
g. Raise questions about need for summarizing, but avoid taking the role himself.
h. Raise process analysis questions, but allow the group freedom to act upon or ignore his comments.

It can be seen from the description in number 9 above that the non-directive discussion leader is most active. The main differences between this behavior and that usually displayed by teachers are that he restricts the number of words he uses in order to provide opportunity for more student participation, (2) listens intently and gives evidence that he is listening, (3) avoids judgmental comments, throwing the decision-making out to the class, (4) shows acceptance of student contribution (this does not mean mere agreement with everything since he is not being the judge), and (5) acts as a model of helpful task and maintenance functions for the group so that students may use these behaviors themselves. Such teacher behavior, of course, requires practice, but the very act of practicing can be an exciting, fulfilling one as the aggregate begins to become a participating group.

Two things need to be underlined at this point. First, the movement of a class from an aggregate to a group is a slow, developmental process. Students are learning communication skills, and this takes time. The teacher who expects an instant change will be disappointed, and disappointment may lead him to fall back on more familiar dominating behavior. If he has patience, however, it will not take the class long to react. Their unspoken question will be, "Do you really mean this behavior, or are you suddenly going to pull the rug out from under us?"

Second, the teacher needs to enlarge his concept of class participation.[5] In the past this has meant the student's saying almost anything, particularly asking the teacher a question to

[5]See comments regarding student participation, p. 81 of this book.

prove he has studied the material and is interested or replying to a direct question from the teacher. In the framework of this book, student participation includes the skillful application of task or maintenance functions when they are needed to help the group solve its problem, or to make a decision, or evaluate what has gone on. In this sense, the teacher's task becomes more complex. He must help to create a supportive environment that will bring students out, *and* he must also help them to sharpen their communication skills so that they become less dependent on his spoonfeeding.

The following dialogue is illustrative of the beginning of a class discussion conducted by a non-directive teacher.

1. TEACHER: For the past week we have been exploring the England of Elizabeth the First. Since it seems hard to discuss anything looking at the backs of people's heads I have moved the desks into a circle. I think we agreed yesterday that we wanted to discuss the developments leading to England's emergence as a world power. Shall we begin?

2. SANDRA: (*After a 15-second silence.*) It feels sort of funny to sit in a circle.

3. TEACHER: (*Smiles*).

4. FRANK: The class looks different.

5. TEACHER: (*Smiles and nods agreement.*)

6. HOWARD: I don't think I've seen some of these people face to face.

7. TEACHER: (*After more silence.*) I am thinking that I agree with Frank. The class does look a little different, but at least *I* usually see everyone's face. I'm wondering how others feel.

---

1. The teacher sets the scene, commenting on the new physical arrangement and reminding class of the discussion question.

3 and 5. Teacher accepts comments, but does not respond, giving other students a chance to comment.

7. Teacher moves from silence to verbal support of expression of feelings, and throws leadership back to group.

---

8.   SUSAN: I like it.

9.   MIKE: It's like Thanksgiving with everyone sitting around the table.

10.   FRED: Boy, you must have a big family.

11.   MIKE: Well, not quite this big.

12.   HARRY: Maybe we ought to get a turkey.

13.   LEE: Let's wait until we get to the Pilgrims.

14.   (*Class laughs and teacher joins in.*)

15.   MIKE: Yeah. We're supposed to be having a discussion.

16.   HOWARD: All right, Mike, go ahead and discuss.

17.   SUSAN: (*To teacher.*) How should we go about it, Mr. Harris?

18.   TEACHER: Well, I guess there are a number of ways to begin, but I'm wondering if we are leaving Mike and Howard hanging.

19.   MIKE: Oh that's all right. Go ahead.

20.   HOWARD: It's not all right with me. How come you cut me off, Susan?

21.   SUSAN: I really hadn't thought about it. Sorry.

22.   TEACHER: It's interesting to me the way groups make decisions. We were talking about how it felt to sit in a circle. Did we need to decide to leave that subject before going on?

23.   FRED: It was Harry's turkey.

24.   HARRY: And then Joe said wait for the Pilgrims.

25.   JEANETTE: And here we are.

26.   MARY: What do we do now?

---

13. Joe's remark served to break the slight tension and to bring the conversation back to the discussion topic.

15 and 16. Mike and Howard picked up on Joe's remark.

17. Susan followed their lead, but threw the lead to teacher.

18. Teacher accepted comment, but made a process comment about whether Mike and Howard had been bypassed.

22. Teacher generalized his earlier process comment to question the decision-making process.

26. Mary asks for direction, and teacher resists urge to tell her.

27.   JACK: I'd like to say something about this circle thing.
28.   HARRY: Go ahead.
29.   JACK: I think it makes it easier to talk.
30.   HOWARD: I hope you don't stop.
31.   JACK: Maybe I won't.
32.   MARY: Should we talk about the topic?
33.   MIKE: (*Humorously.*) We have to make a group decision.
34.   (*Class laughs.*)
35.   HOWARD: Let's agree that anybody can say what they're feeling even if it isn't on the topic.
36.   MARY: But that would be confusing.
37.   MIKE: What do you think, Mr. Harris?
38.   TEACHER: I think it's an interesting idea, though Mary might be right. We need everyone's help in deciding.
39.   MARY: You're not going to tell us the answer?
40.   TEACHER: I'm not sure I know the answer, Mary. Perhaps we should know more about what Howard had in mind.
41.   HARRY: What did you have in mind, Howie?
42.   HOWARD: I just thought we could decide to leave the talk about sitting in a circle, which I'm getting tired of anyway, if we could feel free to return to it like Jack if a thought hit us.
43.   FRED: That sounds all right to me.

---

27. Jack makes comment on circle. From student response, it appears that he is usually silent. They reinforce him (28 and 30).

32. Mary again asks for direction.

33. Mike makes it a joke, but *does* ask for group decision.

35. Howard asks for a group norm.

36. Mary questions it.

37. Mike throws it back to teacher.

38. Teacher asks group.

39. Mary wants clarification.

40. Teacher does not refuse, but helps group to elaborate Howard's idea.

42–43. Howard elaborates and Fred supports.

44.   MARY: I still think it might get confusing, but if Mr. Harris doesn't know the answer, neither do I. I'd be willing to try it.

45. JEANETTE: Fine. Let's get on with it. Now, when the Spanish Armada sailed. . . .

46.   MIKE: Jeanette.

47. JEANETTE: Yes?

48.   MIKE: Seriously, now. I don't want to cut you off, but I don't think the group really made this decision.

49. JEANETTE: Oh, for goodness sake!

50.   JACK: I think he's right, Jeanette. If you start talking before you check the decision, how do you know that anyone's listening?

51. JEANETTE: Well, what do you want me to do?

52.   SUSAN: What I should have done before. Ask everybody if they are ready to discuss the topic.

53. JEANETTE: Okay. (*To class.*) Are we ready to discuss the topic?

54.   MIKE: (*Breaking several seconds of silence.*) I'm ready.

55.   FRED: So am I.

56. (*General murmur of assent with nodding heads.*)

57. JEANETTE: All right. Now, I think we should start with the Armada. When Elizabeth began. . . .

44–45. Mary withdraws her objection and Jeanette begins discussion.

46–52. Mike raises question about group decision and gets Jack's support. Susan shows that she has been thinking about her earlier effort to get discussion started.

53–55. A group decision is made (as well as it can be in this beginning group) and Jeanette begins. (NOTE: teacher has moved into the background, though he will want to check the feelings of students about this at a later time.)

AGREE-DISAGREE EXERCISE

Often teachers wish to know how students feel about the content of the course, how it is being taught, how it might be improved to meet their needs. Such information could be quite valuable to all concerned. While the aggregate is working its way toward group maturity, however, teachers may be reluctant to open up such questions for discussion. And even when they do, the chance of getting anything close to a full group response is quite small. Until a class develops trust that their ideas are really valued, and until students develop some skills in expressing ideas in a constructive way, communication of feelings is difficult. But the process has to begin somewhere, and one method that seems to offer promise is the agree-disagree exercise.

Simply put, this type of exercise consists of a set of written statements concerning a particular area of interest. The student, receiving a copy of the statements, reads them through and indicates his agreement or disagreement with each item.

If ten statements are composed so that five will favor one point of view and five favor another, it is a simple task to determine general attitudes. It is also easy to check student opinions individually and generally.

As is the case with all such data, the teacher may collect the papers for his own purposes. On the other hand, the students themselves may wish to analyze the findings in order to tap the otherwise unexpressed feelings of their peers. As the trust level grows in the class, it is usually wise for the teacher to have students collect, analyze, and report such data.

A more sophisticated use of the device involves an effort to reach consensus in the group. While anyone can, if instructed, indicate agreement *or* disagreement, it is safe to assume that students will have mixed feelings on a number of the items. Thus, the teacher may use the statements in the following way:

1. Announce that the sheets contain a number of statements about X (whatever the subject may be), and that each student is to read them carefully and mark them agree or disagree.

2. After allowing enough time for reading and reacting, divide the class into groups of five. These groups are to arrive at a consensus concerning their agreement or disagreement with each item. They may change the wording in any way that will help them make these decisions.

3. Each group then will report their conclusions to the rest of the class, including their changes in the wording of items and their reasons for making the changes.

4. The teacher may wish to have the entire class reach consensus, or he may end the exercise after the groups have reported and the class has had time to discuss the reports.

This procedure, whether the entire class reaches a consensus or not, brings out clearly the thinking of the students concerning the main issues raised. In addition, it creates a sense of sharing and communicating that will encourage total class participation. Its success will, of course, be enhanced to the degree that the teacher follows through in response to the opinions brought out. Such follow-through should include trying out some of the suggestions *and* allowing more time for expression of feelings at a later date. It would be true to the notion of group growth if the students themselves could conduct the second exercise. By the third or fourth time, the class usually outgrows the need for the exercise and begins to talk more freely.

A specimen of an agree-disagree exercise appears in Figure 13. Examination of the items will show a number of things. First, they are all concerned with questions of class procedure and teacher behavior. Second, they are divided between desires for teacher direction and desires for student direction and freedom. Items 1, 2, 4, 8, and 10 call for teacher direction while items 3, 5, 6, 7 and 9 call for student direction. In addition, item 1 is the opposite of item 5 and item 3 is the opposite of item 8. The opposite items serve to check each other, but also they introduce alternatives for student thinking. Use of this exercise should provoke a great deal of controversy and discussion.

Agree-Disagree Exercise

Read each of the items below carefully and indicate your agreement or disagreement by placing an X on the appropriate line to the left.

Agree   *Disagree*

1. The teacher ought to do all the planning in the course because he knows most about the subject matter.

_____ _____

2. Outside reading should always be handled by having each student turn in a written book report to the teacher.

_____ _____

3. Using student committees for learning and reporting is a valuable part of the course.

_____ _____

4. Lecturing by the teacher is the best way to cover the subject matter.

_____ _____

5. Teachers should allow the students to participate in planning the course work.

_____ _____

6. Students can often learn more from each other than they can from the teacher.

_____ _____

7. Seats should be moved into a circle for class discussions.

_____ _____

8. Committee work wastes too much time. The teacher should do the teaching.

_____ _____

9. It is important that students in a class know each other and have a chance to talk to each other while the class is in session.

_____ _____

10. The teacher should call on people in class when they do not volunteer.

_____ _____

Figure 13.

It is easier to speak freely in small groups than it is in large ones. It is even easier in *very* small groups. A teacher's constant problem is the promotion of full participation in the class which is a very large small group (25–30 seems average). In attempting to deal with this problem, he faces the inhibitions caused by his own behavior, the aggregate status of the class, and the difficulties students have in speaking freely before an audience that may not support or even listen very carefully to what they are saying.

Typical teacher behavior seems to ignore or be unaware of these participation blocks. Instead of waiting until a student makes a contribution and then reinforcing this, a teacher may attempt to draw in silent members by putting them on the spot with a direct question. Since the teacher himself, placed on the receiving end in one of his college classes, could probably do little more than give a quick unthoughtful answer, it is fairly safe to assume that the student will not respond to probing with any change in his usual silent behavior. (It is true that some people *do* need a direct question or comment from the leader to get started, but this procedure is a chancey one to experiment with in the class situation before the aggregate has become a group.)

Besides the obvious problem of embarrassing the student and increasing his silent withdrawal, the teachers move of "pitchforking" students into discussion has a number of other drawbacks. For one thing, it involves rejecting the enthusiastically raised hands of the strong participators who may begin to fall by the wayside from neglect. For another, it reduces the *type* of participating to a series of short responses to teacher questions. Like most of the teacher's classroom behaviors, the recitation lesson stems from his basic concepts (or lack of clear concepts) of how people learn and of how groups interact.

An alternative to the "pitchforking" or "tooth pulling" approach to broader participation is the buzz group. A teacher who wishes to produce an atmosphere in which more students will contribute to a discussion may begin the session by dividing the class into groups of five to explore ideas for ten minutes. At the end of the allotted time, the class reconvenes for a general discussion. Since more people have had an opportunity to speak and to motivate themselves in the buzz session, the notion is that more individual students will contribute in the general discussion.

Buzz groups can be used at the beginning, middle, or end of a class session for a number of purposes. The two models below are illustrative:

Beginning Discussion

1. Either from his own feelings concerning the main points to be discussed, or from the decisions of the class at a previous session, the teacher prepares written guidelines for each participant.

2. At the previous session (to save time if it seems necessary) he explains that the class will begin with ten minutes of small group discussion, and then selects the groups (or lets them select themselves). Each group will be not less than four nor more than six students. Following the ten minutes, the entire class will reconvene to carry on a general discussion, which the small groups have started.

3. (*Notes:* (a) It is not necessary for the buzz groups to come to any conclusions. This is merely a warmup for the class discussion. (b) The written guidelines may be passed out a day ahead so that students will have time to think about the questions.)

4. On the day of the discussion, the teacher directs students to form the buzz groups and begin their discussions. (As the group matures, the students themselves can begin the process. A definite sign of an aggregate is the class that waits to be called to order each time it meets.)

5. Teacher acts as time keeper and calls a halt to the buzz groups at the end of the ten minutes. (During this time, he may wish to sit in on one or more of the groups. And, if he does this, he may wish at some future time to check the impact on students of his joining the group. In the beginning stages, his presence will probably inhibit some students.)

6. After he has called time, the teacher will have the students move their chairs into a total class setting and begin the discussion.

7. (*Notes:* (a) See the description of discussion leader behavior on the preceding pages. (b) After leading this activity two or three times, allow one or two students to be the leaders. (c) Get written or oral student reactions to the procedure. Do they have suggestions for modifying it in any way? (d) Devote some time to process analysis. How well were task functions carried out? Were there efforts at group maintenance?)

THREE STEP DESIGN

It is difficult to maintain the relative openness and spontaneity of the five-member buzz group when the situation abruptly changes to a twenty-five or thirty member discussion. Success in the transition will depend to a great extent on the growth of group maturity and the leader skills of the teacher.

In the initial stages, a three-step process may prove helpful in creating a supportive atmosphere for non-participators.

1. This design will take two 40–50 minute class sessions.
2. The teacher may pass out guide sheets and give instructions a day ahead, or he may do this orienting at the beginning of discussion session one.
3. Teacher sets the stage by passing out sheets and commenting on questions.
4. He then tells the class (e.g., 24 students) that they may discuss the questions in groups of six for ten minutes.
5. At the end of ten minutes, the sixes will combine into two groups of twelve for twenty minutes.
6. At the end of twenty minutes, the groups of twelve will summarize their discussion in written form. (Two written copies will be handed to teacher.)
7. At the following session of the class, the teacher reconvenes the original groups of six for ten minutes, giving each group a copy of the written summaries handed in at the last session of the class.
8. (*Notes:* (a) In this design, the students move more gradually into the total class. (b) On the content level, much work will be done regarding the discussion questions. (c) On the process level, there will be more opportunity for individual participation.)

The teacher should never lose sight of the fact that process awareness and process skills do not occur automatically when people form aggregates of any size. Thus, the student who badly needs support and recognition in order to participate may not be helped very much in a buzz group. In order to help an aggregate grow toward group maturity, the teacher must help the students to be aware of and develop skills in maintenance as well as task functions.[6] In doing this, of course, he should not play down skill development in the task area, since students (from kindergarten through the graduate school) need work in both these sets of functions. (Typically dependent group members tend to supply only initiating behaviors, leaving most of the other task functions to the appointed leader. In the initially unstructured T-Group,[7] members usually feel somewhat lost and helpless when the *Trainer* refuses to take over the stereotype of the chairman role and tell them what to do.)

Brainstorming

A rather specialized technique has been developed in the higher echelons of the American business world, which involves participants in a sometimes breathless process of tapping the idea reservoir of the group. Designed to facilitate problem solving, the activity of *Brainstorming* can easily be adapted to the classroom. The versatility of group brainstorming has been pointed up by Dr. Robert Wilson of Portland State College in Oregon in these words:

> Brainstorming may be used on almost any type of problem. It is especially useful on school and classroom problems such as: What can we do to make our school more interesting and more comfortable? How can we develop better discipline in the playground? How can the line in the lunch room be

[6]See discussion of task and maintenance functions, pp. 58–62 of this book.

[7]For a comprehensive treatment of the T-Group technique of group training see Bradford, Leland P. et al. *T-Group Theory and Laboratory Method: Innovation in Reeducation*. New York: Wiley, 1964.

For participation in T-Group Training, contact National Training Laboratories of the National Education Association, Washington, D.C.

speeded up? What questions would be most interesting to study in this unit?[8]

Though success with the approach will come only through practice, the basic rules are simple to understand:

1. Group size should be about twelve.
2. Subject matter should be in terms of a specific problem.
3. The problem should be one that could be solved in a number of alternative ways. (An either-or question would not be appropriate.)
4. What is sought is a number of ideas. (Questions calling for judgment are not appropriate.)
5. Quantity is called for initially. (Evaluation of ideas come later.)
6. Criticism of ideas is not permitted. (This will come at a later stage.)
7. Participants should feel completely free to throw out any ideas that occur—even the wildest notion is encouraged.
8. Participants should also feel free to build on the ideas expressed by others or to combine any number of previous ideas. (In the jargon of brainstorming, this is called "piggybacking" or "hitchhiking.")
9. Participants should be quite familiar with the problem and with at least the traditional ways it or similar problems have been handled in the past.
10. Wherever possible, it is helpful to "seed" the group with a few experienced "Brainstormers."

Having spent so much of the time of their lives in schoolrooms, students have many feelings about the ways in which classes are conducted and have many ideas for improvement. Unfortunately, independent student thinking is rarely valued by school authority and therefore rarely used by the student. Thus, the brainstorming of ideas may come with difficulty at first and instant success should not be anticipated. If the teacher follows up on the exercise in such a way as to show respect for the ideas proposed, however, subsequent trials will

[8]Osborn, Alex F. *Applied Imagination: Principles and Procedures of Creative Problem-Solving.* New York: Charles Scribner's Sons, 1963, p. 163. This book is an excellent resource in the area of brainstorming.

become more productive. A teacher who can reach the store-house of ideas locked within his students will be rich indeed.

One of the many applications of brainstorming might follow several sessions of student committee work. (Later, as the group becomes more cohesive, the teacher may wish to have the class work on the improvement of *his* teaching, but it may be easier on both parties to begin by having them analyze something *they* have done.) The committee work may be evaluated in a number of ways. Typical of these is the full class discussion led by the teacher who asks, "How can we improve committee work?" The number of ideas volunteered will be related to the freedom felt by individuals in the class to partici-pate openly. Often such a session is limited to the few who characteristically do most of the talking.

An alternative might be to brainstorm the problem, and the procedure might be as follows:

1. At the class session during which the committee work is finished, the teacher announces that the next two sessions of the class will be devoted to the development of ideas that will make committee work more enjoyable and valu-able.

2. For homework, each student is to write three ways in which committee work in the class could be improved.

3. At the class session that concludes the current committee work, the teacher leads a brief discussion concerning stu-dent feeling about the activity.

4. With this discussion as a motivational springboard, the teacher suggests that what is needed is a boxful of ideas, and that they can, if they wish, play a game of idea pro-duction during the next two sessions.

5. Class is divided into two groups with equal numbers of boys and girls in each group. Groups are labelled "A" and "B."

6. At the beginning of the next session, the teacher will col-lect the homework assigned mainly to assure that class members will have done some thinking. The papers are collected because reading from one's paper would destroy the spontaneity of the group session.

7. Two secretaries are selected for each group, their tasks being to write ideas as they are contributed. One will take

the even-numbered ideas while the other will take the odd. This should give them time to keep a running notation in longhand.

8. Teacher will explain that group "A" will begin for 15 minutes with group "B" as observers. Then the groups will reverse roles so that each group will have 15 minutes activity during the session.

9. Rules are that no criticism is allowed. The main purpose is to get out ideas. No idea should be withheld because a person feels it is wild or foolish. Ideas will be judged later. Right now, let's just concentrate on getting them out. It is also part of the game that one may add to the ideas of others or combine two or three ideas into a new one. In this way, the power of the group can be released.

10. Having said this, the teacher seats group "A" in the center of the room in a circle and, after restating the problem, directs them to begin. (The problem is: "How can we improve committee work in this class?")

11. As the group begins, the teacher may have to "prime the pump" by contributing a few ideas. He may begin with one conservative and one wildly liberal idea, being careful not to dominate the session. The homework assignment should be helpful in getting things started.

12. During the session, the teacher acts to enforce the rule of no criticism and to reinforce the norm of anything goes. It is essential to challenge the habit of idea censorship, which inhibits people from free participation.

13. After 15 minutes, the teacher will switch groups and continue for a second session.

14. At the end of the class, the teacher (or a student group) can take the lists of the group secretaries and arrange them for duplication. The duplicated list should be ready for the next class.

15. At the next class, idea lists can be given out to each student and, through class discussion, narrowed down to a few usable ideas, one or more of which can be implemented.

For the purposes of group maturity, brainstorming introduces maintenance emphasis in terms of a reduction in critical comments and because of the norm of reinforcing any and all participation. The exercise itself is motivating because it departs from the usual routine and because it tends to involve most of the students. It should be quite productive in terms of ideas, and it should develop student commitment to carrying out the ideas since the students themselves developed them.

CASE ANALYSIS

A highly motivational device on which a class discussion can be built is the case analysis technique, which has received a good deal of attention and refinement at the Harvard Graduate School of Business Administration. This approach, which can be modified to meet a wide number of classroom objectives, is one of the sharpest attacks yet developed on the "teacher talk–student listen" syndrome of so much current schooling. In conducting a case study, it is the teacher who listens and asks questions; the students define the elements, analyze the problem, propose solutions, and begin to gain confidence in *their* ability to come up with answers.

"A good case is the vehicle by which a chunk of reality is brought into the classroom to be worked over by the class and the instructor."[9] This reality is in the form of a written account of a problem faced by one or more people. Details concerning those involved are provided plus the background leading up to the moment a decision has to be made. The case description usually ends at that point. The members of the class then face the task of analyzing the data in order to develop one or more possible courses of action.

In this process, the outside reality of the case becomes the inside reality of the class as students begin to identify with the characters and bring their own personal felings to bear.

> . . . the children analyze the emotional forces involved, isolate and discuss the conflicts and problems of the people, evaluate their personalities. Then . . . they talk about themselves. Have they ever felt these emotions? What

[9]Andrews, Kenneth R. (ed.). *The Case Method of Teaching Human Relations and Administration.* Cambridge, Mass.: Harvard University Press, 1960, p. 215.

have they done about it? Have they ever faced a similar problem? How did they solve it?[10]

Personal involvement leads to a feeling of coping with reality, and this enhances the learnings in problem-solving skills and in the process of critical thinking. In contrast to other teaching procedures, which seek to impart elements of the scientific method in outline form to be memorized and fed back on written tests, the case method follows the concept of "Learning by doing."

> In most of the cases, one person has to make a decision at the end of the case. The reader should, after reading the case, assume the *position* of the decision-maker. . . . The reader's job is not to try to decide what (the case character) would have done, but to decide what *he* the reader, would do given the circumstances which have led up to the moment of decision.[11]

True to the aim of providing student experiences that will develop self-direction and personal commitment, the classroom analysis of a written case gives initial guidance and structure, but places the burden of thinking, reacting, and reflecting upon the students, where it belongs. Teaching should not consist of the teacher's demonstrating *his* ability to deal with material; but rather in the creation of situations in which students can test out, develop, and evaluate *their* abilities. Typical of student reactions to the case approach are the findings of a study done in teacher training more than thirty years ago: Students involved said:

> Students grow in ability to recognize, analyze, and solve problems in their teaching situations. Students take an active and objective part in their own professional and personal development. Students develop leadership and intelligent followership through the give-and-take relationships set up by this technique.[12]

[10]Bullis, H. Edmund and Emily E. O'Malley. *Human Relations in the Classroom: Course I.* Wilmington, Delaware: The Delaware State Society for Mental Hygiene, 1954, p. 2.

[11]Hodgkinson, Harold L. *Educational Decisions: A Casebook.* Englewood Cliffs, N.J.: Prentice-Hall, Inc., 1963, pp. x–xi.

[12]Sperle, D. Henryetta. *The Case Method Technique in Professional Training.* New York: Bureau of Publications, Teachers College, Columbia University, 1933, p. 66.

It should be understood at the outset that case analysis, or any other approach that tends to introduce change in the norm of the active teacher and the passive students, is *not* the easiest road for the teacher to follow. Use of the method does not guarantee instant success (any more than a lecture or recitation approach might). On the positive side, it has the advantage of being a break in the routine most students have come to expect. In addition, it provides initial structuring on which to base a discussion—the student is provided with a focus for his thinking. And if the case presentation touches areas of his personal experience, he can draw on previous thinking and acting in order to participate in discussion. On the negative side, the student is faced with teacher refusal to play the usual game of telling him what he has read, pointing out the more subtle aspects, doing the job of analysis for him, and finally, telling him the answer. For many students, such an experience is a frustrating one. He has probably had very few learning experiences in which he has really had to think, even fewer in which he has had to interact with his peers, and he may have little confidence that what he says or decides might have validity. A common response after some discussion is a student request that now the teacher tell them the *real* answer.

The teacher's role here, as in every teaching situation, is one of maintaining successfully a delicate balance. On the one hand, he must resist the temptation to give in to dependent students by telling them all the answers (actually, they will not value this type of experience in the long run); on the other hand, he must respond in some helpful way, or increasing anxiety and frustration will diminish student learning. In essence, his goal is to be helpful not in terms of giving answers or doing the students' thinking, but rather in terms of teaching his students how to *get* answers and how to *do* thinking. His goal is a long range one. At some point, the student will no longer have the teacher to guide him—what will he do then? It is part of our folklore that an American private soldier can and does carry on even when officers and non-commissioned officers have been killed. This claim is often set against the behavior of soldiers from more authoritarian cultures who stand helpless and bewildered when their leaders are taken away. Lack of American individual initiative in the Korean "Police Action" has been pointed out, however, as a criticism of the teaching of democracy in American schools. It would be ridiculous to assume that case analysis, or any other teaching method, could magically clear up these problems. If self-direction and the ability to think for one's self is a desirable movement toward solution, however, then this method is one step in the right direction.

Before defining and illustrating case analysis, it would be well to know specifically what the teacher might have in mind when he uses the technique. Following is a list of main emphases, teacher behaviors, and expected outcomes. (The reader should always keep in mind that realistic outcomes of the first experience would be merely that the students learn something about handling such an experience. The general outcomes will probably not be realized until they have repeated the experience several times.)

Main Emphasis

In using case analysis, the teacher will be concerned with the following:

1. Deepening and extending subject matter learning.
2. Student application of previous learnings.
3. Development of skills in critical thinking.
4. Application to subsequent learning.

Teacher Behaviors. In conducting a case analysis session, the teacher will:

1. be non-directive in leading discussion,
2. help students to "see" their approach to dealing with the problem,
3. point out task and maintenance functions,
4. help students see relationships between what they are doing now and previous learnings in the content of the course and in processes of thinking, problem solving, and decision making. (Where a case is used as an introduction, this point would have to be modified),

5. help them determine what further knowledge and understandings they need and what methods of inquiry (reading, researching, interviewing, field trips, guest speakers, etc.) they might use to gain this further knowledge and understanding,

6. help them to summarize and analyze what they have done with their discussion of the case on both content and process levels.

Expected Outcomes. As a result of participating in case analysis, students will:

1. develop more self-direction and willingness to share responsibility for learning with the teacher,

2. display increasing skill in critical thinking, problem solving, and decision making,

3. modify their attitudes toward the subject matter of the case under discussion,

4. increasingly apply previous learnings in dealing with present problems,

5. demonstrate increasing ability to analyze their interactions on both content and process levels. (What have we learned about the subject? What have we learned about improving group problem solving and decision making?),

6. become motivated toward further learning,

7. display increasing confidence in the importance and validity of their own decisions.

Procedure for the case technique includes having students read the case before the discussion session. At the beginning of the session, the teacher opens with a question such as, "What do you see as the problem here?" or "Who would like to begin the discussion?" From that point, he acts to supply needed task or maintenance functions when they are not forthcoming from the students. He does this infrequently and only as a model for the students to pick up and use. It is *their* problem; *their* discussion. The teacher avoids being maneuvered into the role of question answerer or decision maker. While this may be difficult for him and for the students at first, the teacher's attitude of careful listening and his willingness to participate in a clarifying and idea linking manner soon begins to set a norm for participation. After all, the students learned present behaviors such as notetaking and recitation from their teachers.

Certainly there should be a structure for the discussion and the development of a solution or solutions. The question raised in case analysis is whether the source of structure should be the teacher or the students. Of course, this is not really an either-or question. While the teacher, using a case approach, does not supply initial structure, he *does* do everything he can to help students to learn the process of structuring for themselves.

Case analysis may be adapted to a wide variety of teacher objectives in any subject area. For example:

Art:	Decision concerning empha-crn art for hanging in the school.
Business:	Decision on the introduction of a new office practice.
Driver Education:	Decision on the background events leading to an accident.
English:	Decision concerning poetic experience in everyday life.
Foreign Language:	Discussion concerning reluctance to speak a foreign language for fear of sounding silly or foolish.
Home Economics:	Decision concerning career women vs. housewives.
Home Room:	Decision concerning variance in teacher and student views on selection of candidates for student council election.
Industrial Arts:	Decision on craftsmanship vs. planned obsolescence in industrial processes.
Mathematics:	Decision on use of deductive vs. inductive method of learning mathematics.

Music:	Decision concerning emphasis on popular music vs. emphasis on classical music.
Physical Education (Health):	Decision concerning harmful effects of smoking.
Science:	Decision on fluoridation of water supply.
Social Studies:	Decision on use of public welfare monies and policies for those on relief.

Following is an illustration of a case study as it might be used in a foreign language classroom. The first paragraph introduces the teacher and sets up the problem. Paragraph two provides background on the teacher and on how she views the job of teaching. It also adds some data concerning her reactions to certain students.

Case Study

INSTRUCTIONS:

Read this case study carefully. Then read it again. Try to get the situation clearly in mind and the behavior and attitudes of the people involved. Can you put yourself in the position of the teacher? Of one of the students? How will this situation develop? What would you do if you were involved as one of the people discussed or as one of the other students?

Parlez-Vous Français?

Miss Johnson is a teacher of French at Harrington High School. She is liked by the better students in her classes because she knows her subject well, speaks French fluently, and is very much interested in having her students speak it well. Her less able students, however, feel uneasy in her class because of the pressure to speak often in the language. Their defense is to never volunteer, take a long time in answering, and then say as few words as possible. Miss Johnson does not want to call on the better students all the time, but it is obvious that she is unhappy with the response of the others in the class.

She was able to travel in France for a year with her parents when she was a high-school student, and she has visited the country twice while a student at college. She loves the language, and is quite strict about her students' pronunciation. She can't understand anyone who does not share her enthusiasm for the language, and the students who won't even try to speak fluently upset her. Though she tries to hide it, she becomes frustrated and angry when students reply to a ten word question with, "Oui."

Lewis Stanton is one of the less fluent students in Miss Johnson's third period class, and he feels that she should leave him alone. For the past week, he feels she has been picking on him and trying to embarrass him by asking him questions in French. He doesn't mind studying the stuff and taking tests, but he feels sort of silly trying to speak. It's a sort of sissy thing to do, and he is a football player.

116

Miss Johnson is looking forward to Thursday's class. She has been working on Lewis Stanton, one of her more reluctant students, for a week, and she feels she is beginning to reach him. All he needs is a little more pressure, and he will begin to speak the language more spontaneously.

The Thursday class, however, does not go so well. Miss Johnson calls on Lewis several times, and he hangs his head and mumbles. Even when she asks him sharply to speak up, it does no good, and the class is beginning to show the tension. Finally, the bell rings, and the class members race for the door.

After class, Lewis meets Mary Howard and Sam Fenton, two of his classmates.

LEWIS: I'm fed up.

MARY: What are you complaining about now?

LEWIS: What am I complaining about now? French is what I'm complaining about now.

SAM: You don't parlez-vous?

LEWIS: It's all right for you to talk. Miss Johnson leaves you alone.

MARY: You think she's picking on you?

LEWIS: Isn't it obvious?

MARY: Oh, I don't know. I think she wants you to learn.

LEWIS: If she'd leave me alone, maybe I could.

SAM: Maybe you ought to make more of an effort.

LEWIS: But I feel sort of foolish speaking French. It sounds so phoney.

MARY: It's a beautiful language.

LEWIS: Yeah. Maybe for girls.

SAM: Well, what can you do?

LEWIS: I'll tell you what I can do. I can go see the guidance counselor.

SAM: Yeah, I suppose you could do that.

MARY:	I think you're being sort of childish. Why don't you talk to Miss Johnson?
LEWIS:	Oh no you don't. I don't want to fail the course.
SAM:	You know, you may have something there. Maybe a bunch of us ought to go to the guidance counselor.
MARY:	Oh, you're both terrible.
SAM:	Well, what would you suggest?
MARY:	We could bring it up in class.
LEWIS:	I don't know, Mary.
MARY:	I think that's the only fair thing for Miss Johnson. She's really a very nice person.
SAM:	On the other hand, we could just wear her down by not volunteering.
LEWIS:	I don't know what to do, but I feel like doing something.

Paragraph three brings a student into the picture along with *his* reactions to the situation. The next two paragraphs set up a confrontation between teacher and student, and the following dialogue builds toward a decision-making moment. After the students have had an opportunity to read through the case, they may begin their discussion. Some points which they may bring out would include the following:

Miss Johnson

Personally interested and knowledgeable in subject.

Wants students to speak fluently and with exact pronunciation.

Is impatient with inhibited students

Feels that pressure is helpful

Sometimes speaks sharply to students

Seems like a "nice person" to Mary

Lewis Stanton
One of less fluent students
Feels picked on
Athlete
Feels speaking is sissy
Wants to go to guidance counselor

General Situation
Feelings concerning speaking a foreign language
Methods of teaching
Teacher-Student communication

While the points above will probably be brought out in a discussion of the case, it is most possible that other, more unexpected points will be raised. While the teacher will have and should have specific objectives in choosing or writing a case study, he should also be alert to additional areas that students bring up as they project their own feelings into the discussion. As all sensitive teachers do in any teaching situation, the instructor using the case analysis method will wish to define and clarify any bypaths that may be brought up by the students.

IN GENERAL

The exercises and approaches outlined in this chapter may be used separately or in support of each other to provide a stepping stone toward open communication in the classroom. Like any teaching methods, they should be a means of reaching the teacher's objectives. Actually, any teaching, call it traditional, progressive, or any other name, seeks to create a readiness and an ability to learn. Teaching, without the creation of these conditions, is similar to a book in the hands of an illiterate.

CHAPTER

5

Reaction
and
Evaluation
Instruments

IN THE CONCEPTUAL framework of Chapter Two as well as in the
various exercises suggested in Chapter Four, there has been a
continued stress on the importance of growth and development
in learning groups. Such movement toward group maturity becomes ultimately the responsibility of each member, and all
members become involved in continual assessment and modification of learning activities. Relating this to the framework, a
learning group begins with all its member backgrounds plus its
present structure (I: a and b), moves into learning procedures
(II: c and d), assesses these procedures (III: e and f), and
arrives at changed member backgrounds and structure (IV: g
and h). Position IV is then followed by further classroom procedures and the II, III, IV processes begins again.

Step III (Feedback) is a vital part of this procedure. It
can be viewed both as a separate activity and as one step in the
larger procedure of the framework. As a step, it consists of
evaluation by the group of what they have learned about the
subject and about learning. Data gathered in such evaluation
is analyzed and used in the ongoing improvement of the group
and its learning.

As a separate activity, feedback deals with student readiness to participate in the evaluation of class activities. In addition, it involves the development of instruments and techniques for the gathering of data. While any classroom operation calls for data gathering in both content and process levels, the procedures described in this chapter will focus—as does the book—on *process*. Because such focus seems to cause some educators to become fearful that *content* may be slighted, some clarification of process evaluation would seem appropriate at this point.

SUBJECT MATTER AND THE PROCESS OF EDUCATION

When one teaches a course in English, social studies, home economics, industrial arts, or any other curriculum area, a number of considerations arise. First, and most obvious, there is the discipline itself. To use mathematics as an example, there are facts, concepts, operations, problem-solving techniques, and a host of other aspects dealing with the subject of mathematics as a body of knowledge and skills. The teacher's task in this area is to select meaningful parts of the discipline and create experiences that will increase student knowledge, understanding, and skill. This may be viewed as one side—and a very important side—of the coin of education.

On the other side of this coin—also important and often slighted—lies the totality of teacher and student interactions necessary to bridge the gap between teacher teaching and learner learning. These interactions, and the feelings of teacher and students regarding them, constitute the *process* of education as the term is used in this book.

If the analogy holds, both sides of the coin are necessary to constitute a whole. One does not exist without the other, though of course the teacher and the class may choose to ignore process. Ignoring feelings, however, does not make them magically disappear; it merely pushes them underground. And from this underground region they may emerge from time to time creating behavior problems, conflicts in motivation, and blocks to learning.

Feelings, both positive and negative, are always generated by interaction, and good teachers have always dealt with them.

No classroom situation exists without both content and process levels of communication. No one can be said to teach unless he teaches *something,* and no teaching and learning takes place without teachers and learners *behaving* in some fashion toward each other. What data, then, is available for classroom collection? Obviously, material from each side of the coin.

Traditionally, however, most testing and measurement has focussed only on content—student ability to deal with cognitive aspects of the subject matter. The process level—attitudes, beliefs, and feelings of students and teachers toward each other and toward the subject matter—has received little more than perfunctory attention. Student emotional responses and the behavior resulting from them have sometimes been dealt with in terms of "behavior grades," which have seemed to reward silence most heavily. But rarely have emotions been spoken of and dealt with directly in the classroom.[1]

"Classroom participation" is a subject discussed in most methods of teaching texts, but what is expected seems to be a series of responses to teacher questions on the content level. Evaluation of process (e.g., the success with which non-participators are brought into class discussions, the real amount of freedom to express oneself frankly, the rapport or lack of rapport between students and teacher) is done poorly or not at all for a very good reason; it is not taught in the first place.

Yet, if one returns to the analogy of the coin, the teaching of process skills is an integral part of the teaching of subject matter. It is the thesis of the present book that process is part of subject-matter teaching just as research-skills teaching is a part of a research requirement in a subject such as history.

In summary, content evaluation (the material dealt with in traditional achievement testing) is and always will be a vital part of classroom teaching. In the writing of this book it has been assumed that the teacher-reader is prepared as a subject-matter specialist, and that he will have some sophistication in the area of subject-matter achievement evaluation. Evaluation

[1]For a clear non-technical discussion of emotional responses in general terms see Coleman, James C., *Personality Dynamics and Effective Behavior,* Fairlawn, N.J.: Scott, Foresman, 1960 (Chapter VI, "The Dynamics of Adjustive Behavior," particularly pp. 207–210 on the use of feedback information.

of content learning will not, therefore, be considered here. The following material will focus on the evaluation of process learning. It will begin with purposes.

PURPOSES OF PROCESS EVALUATION

Simply put, evaluation is a process of assessing the attainment of objectives, though it may sometimes also be a means of developing them. As a normal course of affairs, teachers plan and carry out plans by (1) deciding on content, objectives, and approach; (2) developing classroom—and out of class—experiences; and (3) using observation, pen-and-paper tests and other data-gathering procedures in order to determine the extent to which their teaching and the students' learning has succeeded.

According to the theoretical framework of page 39, the products of evaluation would be fed back to the students (perhaps *by* the students) in order to focus attention on whatever change has taken place as a result of classroom interaction. This, in turn, would influence the direction, the kind, and the quality of further learning experiences as indicated by the *Cycling Process* of the framework. Inherent in this concept of teaching and learning is that student involvement in the evaluation is, in itself, an important learning activity.

Stemming from this way of viewing evaluation of learning, five purposes of evaluation may be identified: These are:

1. To get evidence that objectives are being achieved.
2. To help students improve self-assessment skills.
3. To obtain data for analysis.
4. To feed analyzed data back into the social system of the classroom.
5. To improve the quality of classroom interaction and, therefore, of learning.

DATA-GATHERING INSTRUMENTS

All of the instruments illustrated and discussed on the following pages have been used successfully in practice and can be used by teachers in their present forms. It should be kept in mind, however, that these instruments were developed in relation to specific objectives (Purposes: #1), and that they can and should be modified to fit the objectives of anyone wishing to employ them. They should also be shared with students who may be involved in their use (Purposes: #2). This would require not only that students respond to the instruments, but that they themselves (perhaps through a student committee) collect the responses, summarize them, report the results to the class, and move toward skills in developing their own instruments in the future.

Several conditions must be met in order that process evaluation successfully develop useful data for analysis (Purposes: #3). First, an atmosphere of mutual trust needs to be developed between students and teacher. If it does not, the students will treat the instruments as a game in which they must tell the teacher what he seems to want to hear, and the teacher, on his part, will be reluctant to share the results of the instruments. Second, the teacher must be open to the possibilities of learning about himself. Although his role differs in many ways from that of the students, he is also a participating group member and, as such, influences the process going on in the class. Third, he must support action to be taken in response to the data (Purposes: #4). And fourth, he must help his students to see that process evaluation is not merely a focus on the teacher's teaching, but that it also includes a scrutiny of the learner's learning. A critical analysis of what is going on in the classroom should deal with learner behavior as well as teacher activity. It seems helpful to repeat the stress on the term *interaction* when dealing with process. A really successful classroom situation depends on *both* teacher and students (Purposes: #5).

Though many research designs are possible,[2] three approaches can be identified in relation to the beginning, the middle, and the end of a learning experience. The first of these would involve the gathering of data at the beginning (a policy

[2] See Miles, Matthew B., *Learning to Work in Groups,* New York: Bureau of Publications, Teachers College, Columbia University, 1959 (Chapter VIII, "Evaluating Training," pp. 223–52). See also Sellitz, Claire, Marie Jahoda, Morton Deutch, and Stuart W. Cook, *Research Methods in Social Relations,* New York: Holt, 1959.

rarely followed in traditional schooling) so that it may be compared with later data in order to determine change. The second design would be to dip occasionally into the ongoing process in order to find out how things are going so that any necessary corrective measures can be taken. The third design is the traditional final examination where the learning experience as a whole is summarized and evaluated.

Two-Step Design

Essentially, this procedure consists of measuring what exists before a learning experience, going through the experience, and measuring it again at the end. If there is appreciable gain in terms of the teacher's objectives when the second measure is taken it may be assumed that it is due to the learning that has taken place. Without the initial measurement, one has no clear-cut data on the state of affairs at the beginning. Where this data does not exist, there may be a question about a high scorer on a final measurement. Did he score high because of the instruction or because he knew the material when he entered the course?

An effective instrument for a two-step design measuring process is the agree-disagree exercise discussed on pp. 98–101. As an illustration, suppose that the teacher develops objectives in terms of (1) increasing student participation, (2) involving students in course planning, and (3) increasing students' interest in the subject matter. One vital ingredient in the attainment of these objectives is student attitude, and an agree-disagree exercise could be constructed with pro and con statements that would give a clear picture of beginning student attitudes. Administration of the same statements at the end of the learning experience would provide data showing whether the learning had altered student attitudes and to what degree. A similar measurement could be made for any set of teacher (or teacher-student) objectives. If this were done for a three-week experience, the data could be shared with the class in order to pinpoint the reasons why there was or was not change in attitudes and what further activities should be carried on in light of the data.

If, for example, there was positive change in all three, it

might be helpful to continue similar classroom approaches. On the other hand, if one or more showed no change or negative change, some investigation and analysis would seem called for. If the problem were centered in student involvement in course planning, probing questions would be, "What is causing the difficulty?" and "What can we do to improve the situation?" Following the implementation of decisions made, a third instrument might be given at the end of the sixth week to determine whether changes in classroom operation have produced any changes in attitudes.

Sociometric techniques,[3] which attempt to chart the relationships of students in the classroom, may also be used in a before-and-after look at process. This technique involves gathering data on student acceptance (and sometimes rejection) of peers, and the charting or diagramming of these feelings. The teacher, then, has a graphic record of those students most accepted, those most ignored, those rejected, and what dyadic or subgroup relationships exist in terms of mutual choice and acceptance. Data is generally gathered by asking the class to list, on a first, second, and third choice basis, students they would want to invite to a class party and to indicate the student they would most like to exclude. This data is then placed on a single sheet of paper with circles and squares representing students and connecting lines with arrows indicating choices. If one imagines a class of seven girls and eight boys asked to make three choices apiece, the data would be assembled as in Figure 14, and the diagram would look like Figure 15.

From the Figure 14 data, one can see that the boys relate (or say they relate) only to the boys and the girls only to the girls with one exception. Rich is the second choice of three girls, and he has chosen Mary as *his* third choice. Gert seems to be the center of attraction for the girls since five out of six chose her in first position. Betty did not choose her, but then no one chose Betty. Her choice of Rich may have to do with her first

<hr />

[3]See Gronlund, Norman E., *Sociometry in the Classroom* New York: Harper, 1959. Also Jennings, Helen H. et al., *Sociometry in Group Relations*, Washington, D.C.: American Council on Education, 1948. Also Moreno, Jacob L., *Who Shall Survive?* New York: Beacon House, 1958.

SOCIOMETRIC CHOICES

Names	First Choice	Second Choice	Third Choice
John	Vern	Fred	Tom
Fred	Mike	Vern	Pete
Mike	Rich	Pete	Fred
Pete	Mike	Rich	Vern
Rich	Mike	Pete	Mary
Vern	Fred	Mike	Rich
Sam	Tom	Vern	Rich
Tom	Sam	Vern	Rich
Gert	Clara	Dot	Mary
Clara	Gert	Dot	Jane
Jane	Gert	Rich	Clara
Mary	Gert	Rich	Clara
Betty	Mary	Rich	Clara
Dot	Gert	Clara	Iris
Iris	Gert	Dot	Jane

Figure 14.

choice of Mary, who seems to have an interrelationship with Rich. It should be stressed that such interpretation of the data must be supported by observation of classroom behavior. The sociogram is only a supplement to the teacher's general feeling for classroom process. However, it does pinpoint relationships, and it often reveals situations not so apparent to the teacher in general classroom operation.

Except for Betty, the girls seem to have a fairly cohesive group with Gert as its focus and, probably, its leader. Iris may be a bit of an outsider since she was chosen only once, and that was Dot's *third* choice.

The boys seem to be formed more into subgroups. Rich, Mike, and Pete are a triad, and Tom and Sam form a dyad. While all members of the triad are chosen at least once by the others, Sam and Tom receive only a single vote and that is the third choice of John, who is himself isolated from the group. Vern may be the group leader except that there may not be much group feeling among the boys to support him. It is interesting that the Tom-Sam dyad votes for him second. But

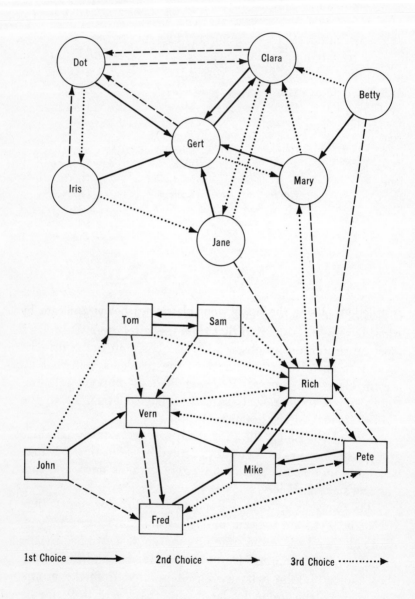

1st Choice ——————▶   2nd Choice ——————▶   3rd Choice ·············▶

Figure 15.

they vote for Rich third, and his support by Mike, Pete, Jane, Mary, and Betty may mean something in terms of his leadership potential. Fred, chosen by Vern, John, and Mike may be a strong independent force. John, like Betty, has not been chosen by anyone. If the teacher has allowed students to sit where they please in class, it would be interesting to check the sociogram against the seating chart.

The imaginative teacher can use sociometric techniques in a number of ways. It is, for example, helpful to know at the beginning of a course who knows whom among the students and how well they know each other. For this purpose, a sheet such as that shown in Figure 16 may be passed out to the class during the first week and a composite picture made as in Figure 17.

The data-gathering sheet shown below in Figure 16 yields

First Street School

Section 8–4   *Miss Daniels*

Instructions: Using the list of your classmates below, indicate by placing an X in the appropriate space which students you know well, slightly, or not at all.

My name is _____.

Class List	Know Well	Know Slightly	Know Not at All
Mary J.			X
Jane P.			X
Freda R.			X
Harriet Q.		X	
John H.			
Michael B.			X
Frederick S.		X	
James T.			X

Figure 16.

a number of choices that can be plotted to form a Composite Picture as in Figure 17 below. This gives the teacher a quick, clear image of who knows whom and who are strangers in the class. Figure 17 shows a group in which there are few close friendships and where most students do not know each other. It is interesting that while Mary is close to both Jane and Harriet, the latter two girls do not indicate that they know each other. Fred and Mike are close, and Fred indicates that he knows most of the people in the class slightly. With the exception of Freda, however, they do not indicate that they know Fred. Freda, while she has no close friends in this class, seems to know most of the students and they seem to know her. James feels that he knows no one at all, but Harriet and Fred feel that they know him slightly. This beginning measurement can be compared to a second taken a month later. The numbers will probably shift to the left somewhat no matter what approach the teacher

Composite Picture
of
Intragroup Relationships

Section 8–4

#	Class List	Know Well	Know Slightly	Know Not at All
1	Mary J.	② ④	③	⑤⑥⑦⑧
2	Jane P.	①	③	④⑤⑥⑦⑧
3	Freda R.		①② ④ ⑥⑦⑧	⑤ ⑧
4	Harriet Q.	①	⑤ ⑧	②③ ⑥⑦
5	John H.		④	①②③ ⑥⑦⑧
6	Michael B.	⑦	③	①② ④⑤ ⑧
7	Frederick S.	⑥	①② ④⑤ ⑧	③
8	James T.			①②③④⑤⑥⑦

Figure 17.

uses. If he seeks group growth and student involvement and if he is successful, there should be an appreciable shift. A record will also exist of those individual students who remain unknowing and unknown.

Data such as that diagrammed in Figure 15 is useful for the teacher, but it is difficult to share with the class, at least in its beginning stages, because of the touchiness of pointing out who has been chosen most or least. As the group matures through time, however, students will become more able to deal with their mutual feelings and more able to express them in helpful ways.

The intragroup relationships data of Figure 17, however, may be shared immediately, and the students can become involved in the planning of ways to increase their knowledge of each other. It has been the experience of the author that students in classes from the elementary through the graduate school do not ordinarily become acquainted with each other in the classroom setting in ways that help them to understand each other and to develop ways of relating. Students *do*, however, develop feelings about each other that affect their learning and the general atmosphere of the class. Often, such feelings tend to be negative, but there is no way to deal with feelings in class situations that stress content levels and ignore process. It is, to a large extent, the near impossibility of dealing with feelings constructively in the average classroom that causes behavior "problems" with the more extroverted students, withdrawal of the more introverted, and premature school leaving on the part of those who tend most to need the schooling experience.

The premise that intragroup relationships, if fostered in the classroom, will enhance learning seems reasonable enough. However, many teachers, brought up themselves in a highly formal manner, are suspicious of any activities that seem irrelevant to the learning of subject matter. They are quite right to be suspicious. Hopefully, of course, they will not use suspicion as an excuse for unwillingness to try new ideas. The collection and analysis of data such as suggested in Figure 17 needs to be done to determine the growth, if any, of intragroup relations. This, in turn, must be checked against measurement

of growth in student motivation and subject matter achievement. If growth in these latter has occurred and it can be
related to growth in group relations, then work on group relations will be seen as a desirable school activity.

Experimental and Control Groups

The discussion above raises an important question concerning the evaluation of classroom process; more precisely, it
raises two questions. The first, and more obvious, concerns the
attainment of process objectives. Is the aggregate becoming
more of a group? Are students *and teacher* getting to know each
other? Are more students participating? Is there a high level of
motivation? Is there an increasing willingness to be open and
constructive in dealing with feelings? Are students becoming
more self-directed? Such objectives need to be carefully measured, and ways must be found to increase the effectiveness of
methodology relating to process learning.

The second question (many would raise it first) is one of
values. Granted that teachers can develop process objectives,
methods of teaching process skills, and ways of measuring
success or failure in reaching the objectives—*why should they
do any of these?* Where do such things fit into the program of
an institution charged with the responsibility for developing
literacy, citizenship, and intellectual growth?

Some answers to this second question have been attempted
in the present volume (pp. 121–22). Others are developed whenever educationists, sociologists, anthropologists, or philosophers
attempt to deal with the role of the school in a rapidly changing society. It is not the purpose here to discuss changing aims
in American schooling. In terms of process evaluation, however,
a few points may be made.

To begin with, process learnings are not separate and apart
from the development of literacy, citizenship, and intellectual
growth. The process of any group (its atmosphere, communication pattern, etc.) directly affects the learning of individuals
within the group. As process is improved, learning is further
enhanced.

This, of course, is a rather broad statement. Does it mean that use of techniques developed in this book will automatically enhance learning? Perhaps. If teaching is, in large part, communication, improvement of communication should improve teaching. But this is still a statement in very general terms. What proof exists for the individual classroom teacher? Probably the best answers for this last question come when the teacher carries on his own research at the local level. For far too long a time, classroom teachers have just "gone ahead and taught." They have ignored to a great extent the research of others (despite mountains of studies on the ineffectiveness of teaching parts of speech, thousands of English teachers go on with such teaching), and they have done little investigation of their own practices.

This last seems necessary, especially if one is to assess the effect of process teaching on content learning. Four ways of going about such assessment are discussed below. The first compares individual students with their own past performances while the other three involve the use of control groups.

Individual Comparison

As the year begins, the teacher gathers pertinent data on each of his students from their past records. (He may wish to delay this for two weeks in order to prevent prejudgment of students.) Information such as I.Q., reading scores, achievement test scores, interest inventories, aptitudes, and school grades—particularly in the subject now being taught—should be collected. Anecdotal records may give the teacher some process data on students in terms of what is usually called "behavior" and "school adjustment."

All of this data is then placed on separate sheets for each student so that changes for this year can be noted. Students scoring very high on past content measures would not be expected to go appreciably higher, but they should not go lower. Students scoring in the middle range or lower *would* be expected to improve. Of course, this achievement is always related to capacity. Process learnings or any other kind of learnings will not make a fast learner out of a slow learner. On the other hand, good process development will tend to bring students closer to their capacities. Even I.Q. scores sometimes change since performance on intelligence tests depends in some degree upon the student's self-image and atttiude toward education. Where these are poor, the I.Q. may not be a true measure. What all of this means is that teachers need, for research purposes, to take a closer look at individual students and their individual learning problems than they usually do.

Such data as a *before* measure on each student can then be checked against present measures. As process learnings develop, each student should begin to feel more supported by both teacher and peers. Some will, of course, be more affected by this than others and give evidence in terms of classroom interest and participation. The teacher can and should run a correlation study between process growth and content growth. Is increased participation linked with higher motivation and higher grades? Do students who enter into the work of the class with more enthusiasm tend to score higher on content tests?

Last Year's Class as Control

The idea of experimenting with one group while using a second group as a control was developed in response to the need to establish cause and effect relationships. One might, for example, use a new method in the teaching of reading and find through testing that students had indeed learned. Was this learning, however, a result of the new method or would it have happened with an older method just as well? The research design would call for the matching of two student groups on the basis of intelligence, reading readiness, maturity, and any other pertinent variables. One group (experimental) would be taught, using the new method, and one group (control) would be taught the way groups had been taught in the past. At the end of the teaching period, both groups would be tested. If the experimental group showed significant differences on the positive side (or on the negative side), it would be fairly safe to assume that the differences were caused by the new method.

One way of doing this in a school situation would be to match students from the teacher's last year's classes with similar students in this year's classes and then compare their achievement. Assuming that a teacher wished to emphasize process learnings during the present year, he might compare one of last year's classes where not much work had been done on process with one of this year's classes where it was emphasized. Since the classes as wholes would probably not be comparable in terms of ability and background, the matched pairs technique would be the only way to make meaningful comparisons.

Concurrent Control Groups

The same procedure may be used with two classes currently being taught. These groups should be matched before the beginning of the school year so that the classes may be compared as classes rather than as sets of individuals.

A factor to be borne in mind with relation to the success or failure of group process is that is is a *group* and not an individual phenomenon. Plus this, the growth of a group lies, to a large extent, in the emotional, non-logical areas of human conduct. This means that in matching groups for evaluation of process, factors of student personality and level of participation are just as important as scores on intelligence and achievement tests.

A design of even more sophistication would be the creation of *two* control groups in addition to the experimental group, or three in all. In this way one would get a broader, more reliable base against which to measure the achievements of the experimental group.

Group as Its Own Control

Because of the difficulties involved in setting up matched groups (these difficulties, incidentally, are not as great as is sometimes thought), the teacher may wish to use a single class as *both* the experimental *and* the control group. One approach might include application of a data-gathering instrument in September to find out whether students knew each other, to what extent, and how important they thought such knowledge would be in relation to their personal learning of subject matter in the course. Following application of this instrument, the class would be taught in the teacher's usual manner for six weeks. Then a second application of the same instrument. Then a second six weeks of instruction this time focussing on process as well as subject matter. Then a third application of the instrument. Since these are the same students with the same teacher, the controls are certainly good. The measurement would consist of determining the differences and direction of differences positive or negative between the first and second testing and between the second and third. The main hypothesis would be that more change would be recorded on testing three in relation to testing two than would appear on testing two in relation to testing one. To add even more weight to the evidence, a fourth and fifth testing ought to be used.

In Summary

Any one or all four of these methods should prove helpful to the teacher who wants some personal reassurance that process learnings at the least do not interfere with subject-matter learning and at best do a great deal to enhance it. All that seems necessary in this respect, in addition to the material above, is a comment and a caution.

The comment is in relation to the split image of the content and process levels of communication. In attempting to do evaluation of process learnings, the teacher should not conceptualize content-matter learning as completely separate and distinct. Nor should he consider the notion of process as something that only happens if the teacher decides to emphasize it. Any group doing anything develops process—ways in which members feel about themselves, the other members, the leader, and the task to be done—and these feelings can have a powerful effect on task accomplishment as a group and as individuals within a group. It is already a standard schooling practice to motivate students and to pay attention to student participation. Process learning merely follows up on these two practices in more specific ways that involve the learner in self-motivation and examination of his own participation plus the participation pattern of the class. In addition—and here it departs somewhat from tradition—it includes a look at the participation of the teacher and what effects, positive and negative, this has on the class.

The caution has to do with how content learning is measured. If content is measured strictly in terms of factual retention, the experimental group should not be expected to score higher (nor lower for that matter). It is when the measurement moves out into the conceptual area, requiring supporting facts and application to new conditions that the experimental group should have an edge. But attempting to measure process learning by the use of a "footnote scholarship" instrument is a poor way to judge its effects. For that matter, it is a poor way to judge content learning.

The notion developed here calls for the teacher first to measure the success or failure of process learning *and then go a step further* and measure the effects of process learning on content learning. (How did learning to deal with our feelings help us to learn history?) And the relationship between process and content learning certainly should be carefully measured.

Measurement sophistication, however, should move teachers off the dead center of the hand-written achievement test. Other questions need exploration. Has participation, motivation, self-direction, or trust level developed noticeably in class? Are students learning *and* applying better or improved ways of communicating with the teacher and with each other? Are previously non-participating students beginning to come out of their shells? Are discussions becoming more effective? And, finally, what amount of content material is retained? An interesting test of method effectiveness might be the administration of the same content test a second time six weeks after the first administration. Here, the hypothesis would be that the experimental group (process and content instruction) would show significantly more retention of learning than would the control group (content instruction alone).

The Gathering of Data

Printed forms for the gathering of group ratings or reactions are, or should be, designed to move from the simple question, "How are we doing?" in the direction of more specific analysis of the situation. This requires a careful definition of precisely what information is needed. An overall reaction on a reactionnaire instrument is similar to a composite grade on a comprehensive test. It *is* helpful in making generalizations, but it is *not* so helpful in pinpointing deficiency areas or in specifying areas that should be improved. In general, then, the printed data gathering form may begin by asking for an overall rating, but it should also include specific questions in specific areas that seem important to the investigator. Where the investigator is interested in student perceptions of the overall experience, an alternative procedure would be to provide five blank lines and require that the student indicate what *he* sees as the specific areas.

Instruments may be *closed end* (where the respondent is asked merely to check a box or circle a number) or *open end* (where the request is for a general comment or an amplification of a previous rating). Closed-end items yield data that can be expressed in clearcut terms such as percentages. It makes for quick and easy communication to be able to read back group responses in terms such as YES 76%; NO 15%; UNDECIDED 9%. Where directions call for circling a number on a 1 to 9 continuum with 1 low and 9 high, data can be reported on this item in a class of 30 as:

$$(1) \; (2) \; (3) \; (4) \; (5) \; (6) \; (7) \; (8) \; (9)$$
$$ 1 \quad 3 \quad 6 \quad 8 \quad 4 \quad 5 \quad 3$$

Open-end items call for student expression of opinion, reasons behind the opinion, or suggestions for improvement. This type response is more difficult to report because it is less rigidly controlled by the instrument. Open-end responses can be, however, quite valuable in the interpretation of quantified data. They serve as specific clues to the interpretation of the 15% NO or 9% UNDECIDED responses, and, of course, they allow the respondents to suggest ways of improvement in their own terms. A middle ground in this area would be first to list five approaches to improvement and have respondents check one or more. Then, in addition, there could be two or three blank spaces for suggestions that do not already appear on the instrument.

Three principles should guide the progress of process evaluation: (1) the teacher should increase his sophistication in the construction of and use of data-gathering instruments; (2) as the class goes on, students should be helped to develop their own instruments; and (3) as the level of trust grows in the class group, there should be a movement toward the open sharing of feelings and opinions so that the crutch of unsigned opinionnaires becomes less necessary.

The following instruments, while they certainly can be used in their present forms, are offered as illustrations of data-gathering methods. As the teacher gains ease and experience, he will want to develop his own instruments keyed to the objectives he and his students have in a particular situation. Items below have been grouped under observation, reaction, self-ratings, and ratings of others.

OBSERVATION OF OTHERS

A number of guides for observing groups in action have been developed in recent years. They range from simple open-ended instructions, as in Figures 8, 9, 10, and 11 of the present text, to more complicated closed end categories such as Figures 18, 19, 20, and 21, which follow.

The interaction analysis categories developed by Flanders (Figure 18) attempt to describe the kinds of communication that occur in the normal classroom. It is highly indicative of the dominating role given to the classroom teacher that seven categories deal with teacher talk while only two deal with the students. Teachers may check the interaction in *their* classrooms by tape recording the class in session and then analyzing the playback or by having a student or a colleague observe the session. The idea of having a student observe the teacher's be-

FLANDERS CATEGORIES FOR INTERACTION ANALYSIS[4]

TEACHER TALK	**INDIRECT INFLUENCE**	1. ACCEPTS FEELING: accepts and clarifies student feelings in nonthreatening manner. Predicts or recalls feelings both positive and negative. 2. PRAISES OR ENCOURAGES: praises or encourages student behavior. Uses humor to release tension, but never at the expense of others. Nods head, says "um hum" or "go on." 3. ACCEPTS OR USES IDEAS OF STUDENTS: clarifies, builds on, or develops student ideas. (May shift to category 5) 4. ASKS QUESTIONS: asks questions about content or procedures with the expectation that students will answer.
	DIRECT INFLUENCE	5. LECTURING: giving facts or opinions about content or procedure; expressing his own ideas, asking rhetorical questions. 6. GIVING DIRECTIONS: directions, commands, or orders. 7. CRITICIZING OR JUSTIFYING AUTHORITY: statements intended to change student behavior to more acceptable pattern; bawling someone out; stating why he is doing what he is doing in a defensive manner.
STUDENT TALK		8. STUDENT TALK-RESPONSE: talk by students in response to teacher. (Teacher has initiated this exchange) 9. STUDENT TALK-INITIATION: talk by students which *they* initiate. (May include teacher calling on student only when this is teacher's response to student's desire to speak. Otherwise, category 4.)
		10. SILENCE OR CONFUSION: pauses, short periods of silence in which communication is blocked or unclear.

There is NO scale implied by these numbers. Each number is intended to classify. It designates a particular kind of communication event. To write these numbers down during an observation is merely to enumerate, not to judge on a value scale.

Figure 18.

[4]See Amidon, E. J. and Ned A. Flanders, *The Role of the Teacher in the Classroom*, Minneapolis: Association for Productive Teaching, 1967, p. 14. This book is most helpfully specific in charting the verbal give and take of the classroom.

Figure 19. CATEGORIES FOR INTERACTION ANALYSIS[5]

NAMES	PETE	JOHN	MARY	FRED	MIKE	JEAN
1. Non-directive leadership. Shares the leadership with others in group						
2. Gets the point of discussion readily. Helps others to understand						
3. Recognizes others, supports their ideas. Disagrees without deflating status						
4. Gives personal feelings and opinions readily. Shows openness.						
5. Participates in an interested manner without dominating.						
6. Clarifies and elaborates own ideas and ideas of others. Summarizes. Orients.						
7. Becomes irrelevant. Gets off track. Expresses irritation and confusion.						
8. Non-participator. Quiet. Withdraws from discussion.						
9. Keeps feelings hidden. Highly task oriented. "Let's get the job done!"						
10. Supports only own ideas. Disagrees with others aggressively.						
11. Constantly questioning the point of the discussion. Does not accept help.						
12. Strong directive leader. Dominates group.						

[5]For another approach to categorizing group interaction see Bales, Robert F., *Interaction Process Analysis: A Method for the Study of Small Groups*, Reading, Massachusetts: Addison-Wesley, 1950.

TASK-MAINTENANCE CHECK LIST

NAMES	Initiating Activity	Requesting Information	Requesting Opinion	Supplying Information	Giving Opinion	Clarifying Elaborating	Testing Consensus	Summarizing	Harmonizing	Facilitating Communication	Accepting Recognizing	Orienting	Blocking
Alice													
Betty													
Clara													
Doris													
Edith													
Frances													
George													
Harold													
Irene													
James													
Kerry													
Larry													
Morris													
Ned													

Figure 20.

CHECK LIST OF TASK BEHAVIORS

Observer Directions: Read through the eight behavioral descriptions below, being sure that you understand each one. As you observe the group in action make a mark in the Number column each time a member employs one of these behaviors. Wherever possible, write the exact words used in the Description column.

Task Behaviors	Number	Description
Defining the group task		
Clarifying and/or Elaborating ideas		
Requesting information or opinion		
Supplying information or opinion		
Making suggestions		
Summarizing discussion		
Orienting—Keeping discussion on track—timekeeping		
Testing consensus		

Figure 21.

havior introduces all sorts of interesting and valuable dynamics into the situation.

It is important to note that these categories exist to describe the interaction taking place. They are not intended as an evaluation. In themselves, the categories do not describe *good* or *bad* behaviors; they merely describe behaviors. These must be measured against teacher objectives and student reactions. If, for example, the teacher's intent is to draw students out in a discussion, and his behaviors fall mostly in categories 5, 6, and 7, then he is not behaving in a manner helpful to the achievement of his stated objectives. If category 10 occurs, it is interesting to note what is done about it. If category 9 hardly ever occurs, the picture would be one of teacher domination and student dependence. If teacher behavior is more heavily weighted toward categories 1 and 2 than it is toward 7 it is probably a happier classroom than if the reverse is true.

Examination of the interaction categories in Figure 19 will reveal that opposite behaviors are described by items 1–12; 2–11; 3–10; 4–9; 5–8; and 6–7. This would suggest that practically all the marks for any single group member would fall either between 1 and 6 *or* between 7 and 12. There may, however, be some crossing of the line as when the dominator (12) clarifies and summarizes (6) and perhaps supports the ideas of others from time to time (3). There may also be some change through time as when a non-participator (8) begins to participate (5).

As with all group observations that describe individual behavior, a rating sheet of this sort must be handled with care when the data is reported. If one is a dominator or a non-participator, one should be made aware of this and its effect on the working group. However, the information must be given in a helpful manner. From the beginning, the group should be made aware that the observation is part of a group self-examination— that the intent is not to label the good guys and the bad guys but rather to develop better group relationships. People who are seen as dominators are usually efficient, knowledgeable leaders. How can the group help them to emphasize this valuable contribution and play down the bossiness that often causes resentment? If John is a quiet non-participator, is this all due to John or is there something about the behavior of the others that is making it more difficult for John to participate? In another group he may be very talkative. Questions such as these can provide fascinating learning opportunities for all members. But there needs to be a degree of group maturity and a willingness to look objectively at one's behavior before such an instrument can be productively used.

The checklist for task and maintenance behaviors (Figure 20) can also be used by one or more observers while a group is in session. The idea, here, is to make a mark in the appropriate box describing the effects of each member's contribution. Making such a structured observation in an effective manner requires practice. If students are to do observations, they should work in pairs or trios in order to cross check each other's observations before reporting the results to the group.

The only critical item here is the last (blocking), and this may be deleted if the teacher feels that such a designation might have a negative effect on the students so described. In many class situations there are a few students whose behavior tends to block the general progress. The other students are acutely aware of this behavior, but they do not know how to handle it, and teachers rarely teach them constructive ways of helping the blocker so that he can learn more helpful and satisfying personal behavior. As a matter of fact, some teachers themselves do not seem to know how to be helpful. As a consequence, blocking behaviors are ignored, treated with sarcasm, or met with aggressive, hostile counterbehavior (sometimes even by the teacher). Therefore, it is potentially quite valuable to deal helpfully with blocking behavior. (Contrast this discussion approach keyed to actual behavior with the practice of keeping a whole class in after school because they were supposed to control the actions of their membership and three of them have incurred the teacher's wrath.)

At any rate, the grid in Figure 20 provides a graphic account of the behaviors present (and absent) in any given group meeting. It pinpoints the frequency of these behaviors, and indicates which members did what (and which were silent).

For a group desiring an objective view of their efforts in getting their assigned job done, the checklist of task behaviors (Figure 21) can be most helpful. The same thing can, of course, be done for maintenance behaviors. (See p. 59 for a listing.)

Here, the emphasis is on the behaviors themselves rather than on the members. This is especially helpful in beginning groups that have not built mutual trust levels. Eight task behaviors are identified, and the observer's task is to note the number of times each behavior appears plus the words used. This last is helpful when the data is reported to the group since it describes in concrete detail how the person went about providing the particular task behavior.

PERSONAL REACTION TO CLASS SESSIONS

In order to involve students in sharing responsibility for classroom success and to get data that either supports present practice or calls for change, the teacher will wish to use occasional reactionnaires. These instruments can be either open- or close-ended or a combination of both. Their items should be keyed to questions that are significant for the particular class at the particular time. Experience will help the teacher to refine the instrument so that it yields data that is of maximum help to him and to the class.

The Class Meeting Reaction sheet (Figure 22) is a simple assessment of overall class reaction to date, specific reaction to today's session, and a request for improvement ideas. The reader will note that this instrument forces the student to look at *his* part in the matter of improvement as well as that of the teacher. No signature is required so that students can feel a bit more freedom to answer frankly. The inclusion of a space for a symbol makes it possible for the teacher to compare later reactions of the same students to determine amount of change.

The two questions call for a 1–7 rating as well as a written comment for each. It should be remembered that students gen-

Class Meeting Reaction

In order to make the class more valuable to you, it would be helpful to know your feelings about what is going on. You need not sign the sheet, but make up a symbol which you can remember and place it on the line provided. You will use this symbol again.

Symbol _____

Circle one number for each question. #1 is extremely low; #7 is extremely high. Explain your rating on the left

My personal reaction to the class is: 1 2 3 4 5 6 7

Comment:

My reaction to this session _____ is: 1 2 3 4 5 6 7
                              (Date)

Comment:

For the class to improve:

I should: The teacher should:

Figure 22.

Post Unit Reaction

Symbol _____

Your frank and thoughtful reactions to the unit of teaching we have just completed should be helpful in evaluating what we have done and in planning for the future.

Circle the appropriate numbers. #1 is extremely low; #7 is extremely high.

My general reaction to this unit is: 1 2 3 4 5 6 7

My interest in the subject is: 1 2 3 4 5 6 7

My feeling about this class as a nice place
   to come to is: 1 2 3 4 5 6 7

The amount of my personal learning in this
   unit was: 1 2 3 4 5 6 7

                                            Too   Too   Just
                                            Much   Little Right

Teacher direction was: 1 2 3 4 5 6 7

                                            Not
As a result of this unit, my ability to par- at all Some Greatly
   ticipate has changed: 1 2 3 4 5 6 7

As a result of this unit, my ability to help
   in planning the course has changed: 1 2 3 4 5 6 7

High spots of the unit were:
   1.
   2.
   3.

Low spots of the unit were:
   1.
   2.
   3.

Figure 23.

Exercise Reaction Sheet

Name _____ Class _____ Group No._____

	Little	Some	A Great Deal			
In terms of subject matter, I learned . . .	1	2	3	4	5	6

	Little	Some	A Great Deal			
In terms of getting to know each other, I know . . .	1	2	3	4	5	6

	Did not Cooperate	Worked together to some extent	Worked quite well			
My group . . .	1	2	3	4	5	6

	Act the same	Change a Little	Change a Great Deal			
If I could repeat the experience, I would . . .	1	2	3	4	5	6

	Little Value	Great Value	Vital			
I now feel that getting to know others in the class is of . . .	1	2	3	4	5	6

	Poor	Good	Excellent			
My overall reaction to the experience was . . .	1	2	3	4	5	6

It could be improved by:

Figure 24.

149

Reactionnaire

Symbol _____

Responding to the questions below will give
you the opportunity to work with your classmates in analyzing and improving the activities of this class.

1. How would you describe your personal activity? (Check one)

Quiet—	Neither quiet	Quite Active
Seldom	nor very active _____	Participating
Participating _____		Frequently _____

2. What has been your reaction to the class thus far? Is it meeting your needs? Why or why not?

3. How could the class be improved?

4. What is on your mind that you wish you could say in class?

Figure 25.

erally do not walk into a class with highly developed critical skills. The teacher will have to teach them how to communicate their personal reactions clearly and helpfully. Perhaps an experience in writing reactions to a film or an assembly program would prepare them for the reaction sheet. Certainly, the teacher should, in discussing the reactions, indicate better ways to respond. Thus, the second reaction sheet should be an improvement over the first as students learn better how to deal with such an assignment.

Much more close ended and detailed is the Post Unit Reaction sheet (Figure 23). The first seven items call only for a 1–7 response, and the small space provided for high and low spots is designed to compress these answers to avoid verbosity.

In evaluating an activity such as role playing or a longer range procedure such as a student committee, the Exercise Reaction sheet (Figure 24) can be helpful in specifying the kind of response the investigator feels is necessary. This is a simple, close ended set of items in terms of student feelings about learning, himself, and the objectives of the activity.

The Reactionnaire (Figure 25) uses the device of the symbol so that this sheet can be compared with others by the same student. It calls for his self-rating in terms of participation and asks for open ended responses to the questions of reaction and improvement suggestions. Question four often gets at significant data by allowing students to express feelings that they have been suppressing.

One of the best ways of handling collection of reaction data is to discuss the problem, the intent, and the way data will be handled with the class prior to passing out the sheets. There should be a willingness and a readiness on the part of the students to take part in such a research procedure. The logical outgrowth of such preparation would be for a student committee to gather, analyze, and report the data. Though they may not be ready for this the first time it is done, they should become involved shortly thereafter. If the teacher always collects and reports the data there may be some suspicion that he is manipulating the responses in order to make them come out with the "right" answers.

Student Self-Ratings

As was noted in Figure 25, the rating of himself in terms of behavior gives a student a chance for some insightful thinking and gives the teacher some clues as to how he sees himself. Since self-concept has such a significant effect on one's continuing efforts to learn, each teacher who considers himself a professional educator must be concerned with this area of student growth. Concern all by itself, however, is not very helpful to the student. Nor is a kindly pat on the back (though such encouragement *is* important). More practical help is afforded when each student is encouraged to look insightfully at himself in terms of debits and credits, allowed to see himself at least partially through the eyes of his peers and teacher, and taught to set personal learning goals *and ways of achieving them*. One way of beginning such a program is through the use of self-reacting instruments.

The Self-Evaluation Checklist (Figure 26) gets at student perceptions of learning in different areas, knowledge of peers and teacher, types of personal behaviors supplied if any, and rating of personal effectiveness. In addition, it reinforces the notion of setting personal goals for learning by asking for a list of these. Such goals should be checked periodically by peers, teacher, and the student himself. As he experiments with behavior calculated to attain these goals, he will probably find that his initial statements have to be refined and rewritten. This, in itself, is an important part of the entire process.

A Profile of Me (Figure 27) moves further away from the work of this specific class and into general self-feelings. The final three items, which the student himself may fill in, often provide insight into personal concerns. Added directions for this instrument might include the circling of the three items that seem most important or most difficult for the student. Also, he may be asked to write a page or two about his feelings as a student in the school, which can be attached to the instrument.

Self-Evaluation Checklist

Symbol _____

	Very Little	Some- what	Fairly Much	Quite a bit	Very Much
1. Were you interested in this unit?	___	___	___	___	___
2. Did you learn content?	___	___	___	___	___
3. Did you learn process?	___	___	___	___	___
4. Did you learn about yourself?	___	___	___	___	___
5. Do you know fellow students better?	___	___	___	___	___
6. Do you know the teacher better?	___	___	___	___	___
7. Did you participate?	___	___	___	___	___
8. Did you contribute task behaviors?	___	___	___	___	___
9. Did you contribute maintenance be- haviors?	___	___	___	___	___
10. How influential were you?	___	___	___	___	___

11. You have been asked to develop personal goals for learning. List below the first three of these goals which come to mind.

A.

B.

C.

Figure 26.

A Profile of Me

Symbol _____

How would you rate: (circle number) (#1 = low #8 = high)

1. Your intelligence — 1 2 3 4 5 6 7 8

2. Your reading ability — 1 2 3 4 5 6 7 8

3. Your ability to express ideas clearly — 1 2 3 4 5 6 7 8

4. Your amount of participation in class — 1 2 3 4 5 6 7 8

5. Your ability to get along with fellow students in committee or other group work — 1 2 3 4 5 6 7 8

6. Your ability to get along with teachers — 1 2 3 4 5 6 7 8

7. Your group leadership ability — 1 2 3 4 5 6 7 8

8. Your ability to keep up with the work of this class — 1 2 3 4 5 6 7 8

9. Your tendency to listen to what the other fellow says — 1 2 3 4 5 6 7 8

10. Your tendency to recognize and support others in a group situation — 1 2 3 4 5 6 7 8

11. Your tendency to impress fellow students as a very worthwhile person — 1 2 3 4 5 6 7 8

12. Your tendency to impress teachers as a very worthwhile person — 1 2 3 4 5 6 7 8

13. Your impression of yourself as a very worthwhile person — 1 2 3 4 5 6 7 8

*What are three important things about
you which are not listed above?*

14. — 1 2 3 4 5 6 7 8

15. — 1 2 3 4 5 6 7 8

16. — 1 2 3 4 5 6 7 8

Figure 27.

RATINGS OF OTHERS

A group matures and becomes cohesive as members learn ways of sharing their feelings with each other in helpful ways. These feelings develop as the course moves along, and they focus on certain behaviors. If feelings—particularly negative feelings—toward the behavior of others are not shared and dealt with, they will be expressed in destructive rather than constructive ways.

Both teacher and students are concerned, and often disturbed, by the non-participator, who sits and says nothing, the over-participator, who is always talking even when he has nothing to say, the "boss," who tells others what to do in an authoritarian manner, and the egoist, who never seems to listen to anyone else because he is too busy paying attention to himself. Both teacher and students are concerned, but in the usual class setting, only the teacher is expected to act. Since it is also usual for the teacher to be outside the group rather than a member, the whole operation of modifying behaviors is made unnecessarily difficult. What is needed is a way of helping students to share with each other their feelings about each other. The following instruments may constitute a beginning in this direction.

Responses to Who Are These People (Figure 28) can be used to share positive student perceptions. Items focus on listening, helping, providing interest and ideas, getting the job done and making it enjoyable. Not only will the students named in these categories feel good about it, but these qualities will be reinforced as students read them and think about them.

Negative qualities are dealt with in gentle terms in order to avoid putting people on the defensive. Such items as very quiet and strong leader, tell others what to do, and even the business of getting the job done can bring out mixed negative and positive reactions in others. Discussions based on the instrument can develop personal insights and group accord.

The reactionnaire can be given to class committees who wish to improve their work. Data can be collected by the

Who Are These People?

Directions: Read each description below and write the name of the student(s) it describes in the space to the right. It is possible that some names will not appear in any of these descriptions.

Symbol _____

Who is very quiet but seems to be trying? _____

Who is a strong leader with many good ideas? _____

Who is most willing to listen to the ideas of others? _____

Who can explain best to those who do not understand? _____

Who shows a serious interest in the work of the class without overdoing it? _____

Who likes to tell others what to do? _____

Who likes to be told what to do? _____

Who would you pick to see that the job gets done? _____

Who would you pick to make sure the group enjoyed itself? _____

Figure 28.

teacher and fed back to individuals. Where the group has more cohesion and trust, a better procedure would be three minutes to react to the sheet followed by twenty minutes of sharing the data orally in small groups followed by twenty-five minutes of general class discussion concerning group building behaviors.

Where this has been done by the author, typical comments in the small groups include:

"Well, Marty, you're a strong leader with good ideas all right, and I'm glad you're in my group. But do you ever listen to *my* ideas?"

"I always look to Sam to explain things. Even the teacher sometimes confuses me, but Sam can always straighten me out."

"Janice, I know you've got a lot of good things to tell the group, but you just sit there. And I think, 'How can I help her? What can I do to get her to talk? Am I doing anything to prevent her?' "

It should not tax one's imagination to guess at the impact such discussions have on students and on the class as a whole. People begin to be interested in classmates and in the subject matter to be learned. Students slowly begin to listen to each other and to see the class as more real and less of a perfunctory game ending in the Friday test, which is crammed for and promptly forgotten.

Both process *and* content form the subject of the Post Meeting Reaction sheet (Figure 29). This sheet is given following the teaching of the concepts of content and process and immediately following a general class session or a committee meeting. Three main purposes are served. First, each student is forced to summarize what has just gone on, which should help his learning and retention. Second, he must look analytically at the process of the meeting as well as its content. Third, he must look at his own behavior in addition to his reaction. This third item is part of the teacher's movement toward having students share the responsibility for good learning experiences.

Group Report Reaction (Figure 30) provides helpful feedback for the group doing a report so that they may improve

Post Meeting Reaction Sheet

Symbol _____ Date _____ Group No. _____

We have talked in class about CONTENT and PROCESS levels of communication. *Both* are *Important*.

CONTENT: The topic of conversation
The subject matter
What is talked about

PROCESS: Who says what to whom? Do people listen to each other? What is the leadership pattern? How do you feel in the group? How do members feel about the group?

Briefly describe content of session. Briefly describe process.

| | |
| | |

| What was your personal reaction to session? | What was your role? |
| | |

Figure 29.

Members: Symbol _____

1. _____   2. _____   3. _____
4. _____   5. _____   6. _____

Topic:
Rate the following by circling the appropriate number. #1 is
very poor; #7 is excellent.

Content: (Was this of help to you? Did it
          extend your knowledge of the area?)   1 2 3 4 5 6 7
    Comment:

Presentation: (Did the group hold your in-
               terest? Was the report
               clear and logical?)   1 2 3 4 5 6 7
    Comment:

Improvement: (How could the presentation
    have been improved? Rate low if it needs
    a great deal of improvement and high if it
    needs little.)   1 2 3 4 5 6 7

Figure 30.

their operation. This is a vital activity since much classroom committee work is abandoned merely because it does not work perfectly the first time it is tried. Both teacher and students should realize that effective committee work needs to be learned through increasingly improved practice. That time spent in such learning is more than justified seems quite obvious when one considers how much work is done in committees throughout the culture and how ineffective most of this work turns out. At this point, the reader might reflect on *his* last committee participation.

In addition to providing feedback for the committees, this instrument allows each student to summarize his learnings and to develop skill in analysis of organization and presentation skills. A student who has carefully criticized a committee should tend to avoid the same mistakes when he himself becomes a member of a committee.

By reacting to the Group Evaluation (Figure 31) the student is analyzing his own group of which he is a member. How well is the group progressing? What, in my opinion, are its problems? How effective am I? How can I do more to help the group? These questions develop analysis of the group without allowing the student to stand back and ignore his own membership. Too often, a member speaks of his group in terms of what those guys are doing well or doing poorly. A major step in his learning comes when he is able to look at the group and include himself and his behavior in the general reaction.

Another potentially valuable area developed in the instrument is that of the teacher's behavior. How much is the group helped by his actions and how could he behave to be even more helpful?

Following up on the notion that evaluation during the learning is as necessary as evaluation following the learning, the Group Progress Check (Figure 32) does two things. First, it calls for a summary not only of what has been discussed and what resources are needed but also a record of action to be taken. Second, it clarifies the perceptions of the members as to what is going on. When six members of a committee all write a different account of what has been discussed, the group learns

Group Evaluation

Symbol _____ Date _____ Group No. _____

	Poor	Fair	?	Good	Excellent
My general reaction to the experience	1	2	3	4	5
Efficiency of group in doing job	1	2	3	4	5
Involvement of members in doing job	1	2	3	4	5
How effective was I?	1	2	3	4	5

Problems in group as I see them.	What I can do to help?

How effective is the teacher?	1	2	3	4	5

How could he better meet the needs of myself and the class?

Figure 31.

Group Progress Check

Symbol _____ Topic _____ Date _____ Group _____

Members Present

_____   _____   _____

_____   _____   _____

Main Areas Discussed	Action

Resources Needed (people, materials, films)	Action

Figure 32.

something about the dangers of assuming that everyone has the same picture.

EVALUATION AND REACTION IN GENERAL

This chapter has been an attempt to further define the notion of a process level of communication in the classroom. It has included a discussion of the content level as well as process, and it has moved into the area of process evaluation. In this latter area, procedures and instruments have been suggested for the gathering and analysis of data. Finally, it has been noted that each teacher (and class) will set certain objectives that seem important to the particular situation. Thus, the material presented in this chapter will need to be adapted to individual purposes.

This is an age of physical and psychological school dropouts, underachieving students, disadvantaged learners, and societal dropouts in the form of teenie boppers and hippies. It is an age of tremendous cultural and academic pressure resulting from unsettled world conditions, a population explosion, and a knowledge explosion. Educators are struggling to teach more things to more people for a longer period of their lives. At a pace bewildering even to the teachers, schools are attempting to cope with the new math, the new science, the structural linguistic approach to grammar, the extension of social studies from a narrow framework of history teaching toward the inclusion of sociology, anthropology plus the expanding spectrum of the behavioral sciences, the development of language laboratories and teaching machines, and the expansion of programs of human relations and sex education.

One resultant of these multi-directional explosions has been a breakdown of—or more precisely a failure to build up— effective patterns of communication in the classroom. And simultaneously with this failure has come increased student demand for identification and recognition within schooling frameworks. The famous Berkeley campus riots were caused, in great part, by student feelings of a lack of personal involvement in the university culture.

To paraphrase a familiar quotation, "Man does not live by content alone." Just as medicine advanced from a group of barbers' apprentices to the highly specialized practitioners of today, education must move in response to current demands. What has been missing in the modern teacher's preparation is a methodology for the improvement of communication. We must reach students before we can teach them, and we must help them to reach us on increasingly effective and mature levels.

CHAPTER

6

Process Communication and the Role of the School

IF THE INTENT of the preceding chapters has been realized, there may be no need for a sixth. The reader can draw various threads together into a garment and make the decision for himself to wear it or discard it.

Since, however, there is a human tendency toward closure, some things should perhaps be said at this point regarding the book, its emphasis, and the educating of emotions as well as intellect. The main focus has been on affect—or process communication—in the classroom.

TRADITIONAL TREATMENT OF SCHOOL PROBLEMS

Historically, in education, those who have written concerning teaching and learning have dealt with such things as CONTENT (subject matter consisting of teacher planned—or textbook planned—ground to be covered); CONTENT MASTERS (teachers fairly well equipped in a separate subject discipline through a four-year college cram course and usually poorly equipped for the give and take of classroom interaction); CONTENT COMMUNICATION (teaching methods that have changed only slightly through the centuries, tending to be one-way affairs with students on the receiving end); CONTENT CAPSULATION (physical plant, usually the "egg crate school" with every room equipped for one teacher-speaker and thirty student-listeners); and CONTENT MASTERY (a hodge-podge of facts, concepts, and skills served up cafeteria style—or, more precisely, army mess style—and occasionally seasoned in haphazard fashion with ill-defined globs of "creative thinking" sprinkled with bits of "how to study." That such an easily criticized operation is allowed to limp along from year to year is a credit to the rigidity of those who direct the American educational enterprise, but it may also be traced to inadequacies in teacher training.

Teacher-as-Subject-Centered-Expert

In the virtual absence of school-based inservice programs, which concentrate on improvement of the teaching act, classroom content masters must rely on their pre-service instruction in the teachers' colleges plus their own empirical experience with students.

Pre-service instruction in teaching methodology, however, has been notoriously poor. Too often it has consisted mainly of professors talking to passive, seated students about discipline, motivation, and a handful of teaching approaches while the professors themselves use the lecture method at its traditional worst. The "student teaching" experience is often a brief six to ten week affair in which the threat of a grade inhibits the pre-service teacher in trying out non-traditional approaches.

Finally, after having survived the ordeal of professional education, the young practitioner, whose most intensive learning has been in mocking and discrediting his own "education" courses, goes forth into a real live school. Here, he is advised by "seasoned" teachers to "forget all you heard about teaching in college." The teaching game, he is told, consists of gaining the upper hand at the beginning and maintaining it desperately in the face of the fighting subgroup called students. He hears—and usually listens to—advice such as: "Start off rough. You can always ease up." "Don't smile until Christmas if you want to maintain discipline." "Don't be friendly with your students or they'll take advantage. They're here to learn; not to make friends."

Operating without a clearcut operational theory of teaching and learning, with a pre-service background that emphasizes *what* to teach rather than *how* to teach, and within a school environment that discourages close supervision and on-the-job improvement, the "modern" teacher is to be congratulated that the quality of teaching in the United States is as high as it is. Much good teaching is going on at present, particularly with that percentage of students who happen to be self-motivated and supported by a stable home background. These students may not be learning to think or to express themselves independently, but they *are* able to use the scholarship of the teacher as they would a good text or film.

With the growing complexity of the society, however, and the school-related problems stemming from such complexity, the concept of teacher-as-subject-centered-expert is proving increasingly inadequate. Students of today need less domination and more personal attention. This has been recognized by the school, but only in its usual traditional, departmentalized way.

Guidance Services

Beginning with the closing years of the 19th century, and developing rapidly in the years following the Second World War, the concept of guidance as a legitimate responsibility of the school has gained continued acceptance. The traditional response, of course, has been to build an out-of-class organization of non-teaching counselors. This has further supported the separation of content and process. In theory, it allows for the meeting of student emotional needs without interrupting the subject-centered emphasis of the classroom teacher. In practice, the guidance counselor in the guidance office with a formidable client load and never enough time cannot deal with student classroom problems as well as the classroom teacher might.

Guidance services have made a significant contribution,

however, in spite of the difficulties imposed by their extracurricular organization. Beginning with the usual stress on academic and vocational help, guidance people have made a rapid movement toward emotional and social counseling. In this they have been aided by school psychologists, social workers, and even an occasional psychiatrist.

All of these developments have followed a changing concept of school responsibility in the face of a changing culture and the difficulties inherent in the challenge of "education for all." They have been an extremely valuable addition to the organization of formal education. Yet, at their best, they can deal effectively only with a small percentage of emotionally exceptional children beyond the reach of the classroom teacher in the classroom setting. They do not and cannot deal with process communication in the classroom since by its very nature it has an immediacy related to the time and place of its occurrence. Such communication needs must be met at the time they are happening. To tell the student to report to the guidance office next Wednesday does not seem a very helpful response.

Isolation of Student Needs

Attempts to ignore the immediacy of classroom dynamics and to concentrate on meeting a variety of needs as if they could really be isolated are still being made by teachers who seem to think that people can be compartmentalized the way knowledge has been isolated in the separate subject curriculum. In this system, the classroom teacher takes care of one's intellect, guidance counselors of one's emotions, assistant principals of one's discipline, and the extracurricular program of one's social needs.

Such separation of needs makes sense when they are to be analyzed in discussion or in a text book, but in action they need to be put back together. A carburetor, a fuel pump, and a fan belt may be taken out of the car for demonstration purposes, but it is absurd to think of them operating separately.

In similar fashion, content and process communication may be analyzed separately for discussion, yet attempting to deal with them separately at different times and different places in a school situation would be like agreeing to use the fuel pump without the carburetor today and the carburetor without the fuel pump tomorrow or to say that this Saturday we will play without the line.

The coach knows that he has to use both the line *and* the backfield. In addition, he knows that certain linemen can receive a pass like a backfielder and that some backfielders can be used in ways similar to the line. This has a parallel in verbal interaction since various human needs not only occur simultaneously, but also overlap and intertwine. This suggests that the concept of intellectual growth is a more complicated one than teachers, or the teachers of teachers, have recognized. Members and leaders of task-centered groups know that people have social and emotional needs, but they have worked, historically, under the assumption that these needs have no direct bearing on the accomplishment of the task. Thus such needs tend to be ignored in the group, and the result is the psychological dropping out of an appreciable number of group members while the rest do most of the work. Such inefficiency, when it is recognized, is blamed on a vague scapegoat called committee work, about which countless jokes have been made (a camel is something that was put together by a committee).

Reports and Labels

Teachers, too, are aware (at least on the intellectual level) of social needs, but they have also operated on the assumption that these have little to do with classroom learning. When failure to deal with these needs results in learning disorders, the school reacts with institutionally approved moves that neatly avoid the main issue.

Report cards and letters sent home urging parents to apply vaguely understood pressures usually increase rather than solve the problem. Children are assigned categories such as *unmotivated, underachiever, behavior problem* and are referred to non-classroom areas for help. Inherent in the material of previous chapters is the idea that most of these students might benefit most by help given in the ongoing context of the class interaction. Guidance and other areas should be used *in conjunction with* and not apart from the classroom. To implement this concept, the guidance counselor might be invited to visit the classroom. His expertese should be available to both teacher and students, and he should not be segregated constantly in a guidance office.

In the magnificent effort of the society to educate all its youth, many serious personality problems are bound to occur, and it would be arrant nonsense to claim that the *process* techniques suggested in the present volume constitute a panacea. But it would be even more foolish to ignore them merely because they do not solve all problems. Techniques for the development of cognitive—or *content*—communication sometimes fail, but the response to such failure has usually been to seek new ways and to improve the old. The same response ought to hold for *process* communication. When teachers realize fully that process and content are not separate and distinct, but rather form two halves of a whole called learning, many of the serious problems of schooling will begin to be solved.

PROCESS IN TEACHING

A summary of process communication in teaching should include a definition, a rationale, and some final comments on the implementation of the program.

Content and Process

While content level has to do with the topic under discussion, process level concerns feelings that group members have about themselves and about others while the topic is being discussed. As has been seen in earlier chapters, the process level is more hidden and more subtle than the content level. People generally have great difficulty in communicating feelings in a group setting, and the typical norm of the task-centered group is that expressions of feelings are not relevant *and should be withheld.*

All of this is perfectly clear and understandable. The American culture, in general, rejects emotional communication except under certain circumscribed conditions such as moonlight and romance. Sweethearts who embrace passionately on Times Square at noon would have sanctions employed against them to alter this overt behavior. A student in a class who turns to speak to a neighbor would call down the immediate wrath of his teacher, and this would be a one-way communication since the student is never allowed to respond in kind. According to prevailing norms, the teacher may express anger through nagging, raised voice, or sarcasm, but let the student reply in anger and the sanctions of the whole schooling institution move in to cut off the response.

It is the cutting off of the response that is unhealthy, and yet free expression might not constitute a helpful alternative. Social class norms dealing with expression of strong emotions provide an interesting parallel. The mother of the *middle-class* child involved in an argument with his peers will tell him to use reason in winning his point or to walk away without losing his temper. In a similar situation, the *lower-class* mother might encourage him to hit the other children and not let them push him around. Here, we see conflict avoidance compared to conflict seeking. In a school situation with a *middle-class teacher* and a *lower-class youngster* involved in a conflict situation there is a frustrating clash of values. The frustration occurs because neither side can give vent to their feelings. The teacher, of course, has a little more freedom because of his authority, but reliance on the use of institutional force or on the choking off of free expression does not reduce the basic frustration. It merely bypasses the problem, and it is this failure to really face issues and resolve them that causes much of the blocking behavior found in the learning group.

Such problems lie within the process level of communication. They have nothing directly to do with the learning or the teaching of subject matter, yet they do exist and they influence the quality of learning and teaching. An irate teacher or a humiliated student cannot merely shed personal feelings like old sweaters and "get down to business." They need to explore their feelings toward themselves and each other.

Though personality clashes and behavior problems provide classroom process problems, they make up only a small percentage of process communication. The bulk of it is less upsetting and spectacular. One common problem, for example, is the lack of free response on the part of students. When the teacher asks Johnny a question he is liable, on the basis of past experience, to feel that he is being put on the spot. Instead of taking the teacher's question as an invitation to explore a content problem, the student often feels that he must recite in order to prove that he has done his homework. Thus, the quality of teacher-student interaction often has a strained, artificial overtone. As for the quality of student-student interaction, they have so little practice in traditional teacher-dominated school settings, that they frequently are at a complete loss when required to carry on a class discussion. It is extremely difficult to make a group of efficient talkers out of students who have been conditioned for years to be highly dependent listeners.

Such problems have occurred, are occurring, and will continue to occur in classrooms. The question raised here is really one of alternatives. What responses are most promising? Which would yield the least frustration and the most conflict resolution? What positive middle positions exist between too much teacher control and too much student freedom? How can students learn effective ways of sharing with the teacher the responsibility for their learning?

Rationale for the Teaching of Process Skills

Since teaching is primarily communication, and since any communication has its content *and* process levels, improvement of teaching is directly related to improvement of communication on both these levels. Because one level is interrelated with the other, the bypassing or ignoring of the process level creates a more serious impediment to learning than has been realized until recent years. Proceeding from the assumption that process must be recognized and dealt with, techniques such as those in the present volume have been and are being developed to improve student-teacher interaction within the classroom setting.

If classroom interaction is ever to raise itself from a sort of non-life gameplaying, the actors on its stage are going to have to recognize themselves and the others as persons rather than objects. As should be apparent to readers of the first few chapters, however, this recognition does not come about merely through good will and determination; it requires time and the development of skills. Basic socialization processes of our culture, aided and abetted by the content preoccupation of the schools, have conditioned both students and their teachers to accept an individualized, over-intellectualized, non-emotional approach within what appears to be a group setting. The change of such expectations—or the reconditioning of the participants—requires time and patience, but most of all the development of communication skills on the process level.

Time and patience—and belief in the ends being sought—are necessary because it is not enough for the teacher to announce that students are free to express themselves in this course and that they are expected to play a part in planning it, carrying it on, and evaluating it. Conditioned to play passive, listening roles, the students will not know how to use freedom and partnership with the teacher in an efficient manner. In the early stages, they will be frustrated by their inability to make group decisions and to deal competently with the subject matter in terms of defining areas of inquiry, locating resources, and using these resources. But this very frustration will generate process that can be looked at. Frustration, like any other communication problem, needs to be faced rather than avoided.

In the solving of communication problems, students will be moving from an aggregate to a group that will include the teacher as a special member. Far from losing control and respect, the teacher will be seen as *the* most valuable group resource. The class will gradually improve in its ability to make group decisions and to set group norms of behavior. When the group accepts the freedom to develop its own norms, it will also accept the responsibility for their enforcement. The teacher will move further toward playing the role of guide to intellectual growth and further away from playing the role of law enforcement officer. The possibilities for human fulfillment in such a group setting are most exciting. Anyone who has experienced a really free atmosphere where responsibility for control and direction are shared and where individual dignity is enhanced would never vote for a return to the baby-sitting nagging going on in too many of today's classrooms.

Changing Behavioral Norms

In the preceding paragraphs the stress has been on (1) breaking the game-playing atmosphere to create a reality situation, (2) changing student-dependency norms, (3) helping to create an atmosphere that will reward the free expression of feelings, (4) developing shared responsibility in addition to shared freedom, and (5) creating a readiness for subject matter learning. The purposes of the exercises detailed in the book deal with bridging the gap between the changing norms of communication. As the teaching year progresses, the exercises— as crutches—become less necessary, and the group, having become indeed a group, can address itself to the improvement of content communication. The assumption here is that process communication needs to be dealt with *before effective* content communication can take place.

The reader will note that both the words *before* and *effective* are italicized in the sentence above. The statement should *not* be read to mean that a class in history should wait for two months before beginning to learn history so that process skills can be developed. Initial efforts to learn history should begin, if not on the first day, certainly during the first week. Process and content skills should be developed together. The point made in the previous paragraph is that initial efforts on *both* levels need to be improved before effectiveness is achieved. Perhaps a better way to put it would be that both process and content communication need to be dealt with as methods of communication before effective teaching and learning can result.

This is similar to saying that communication must be improved before we can have improved communication. Such a statement could be dismissed as belaboring the obvious if it were not for the fact that communication in learning has, historically, been seen as primarily content-centered. What is new here is the focus on process communication *in addition to and combined with* content focus.

A subtle understanding problem seems to be caused by efforts—such as those in the present volume—to isolate process communication for the sake of studying it and proposing techniques to improve it. In so doing, there is the danger that it begins to be thought of as something separate and distinct from teaching the subject. Once this is done, the teacher may see it as something of a chore added to an already full day. Given a choice, he may choose to ignore it as so many teachers have done before him. In actuality, however, there is no choice. Process exists, and no one really ignores it. Whenever human beings come together to do a job such as that of the classroom they generate feelings about the job, about themselves, and about the others who are present. They may not bring these feelings out in the open where they can be handled, but the feelings are there nonetheless; they cannot be completely ignored. The basic question is not whether process should be dealt with; rather, it is *how* it should be handled.

Aspects of Classroom Process

When one contrasts an American classroom with one in present-day western Europe it becomes apparent that Americans deal more with process in the school. On the other hand, teachers in western Europe are dealing more with process than did their predecessors of past generations. There seems to be a world-wide movement (evident in areas such as India as well as in the West) toward bringing the teacher more into the give-and-take of the learning group. American schools, influenced by changes in the American culture and by educational philosophers such as John Dewey, have made giant strides toward permissiveness in the classroom and recognition of the "whole child" concept. Yet even in the U.S.A. progress has been slow. There has been a fear that freedom of student expression would result in anarchy. And this is a real problem when the teacher and students lack process skills. Allowing students freedom of expression is not really *dealing* with process; it is merely the removal of rigid controls. If substitute controls are not developed rapidly there can be classroom behavior problems. It is the failure to establish democratic controls that has caused most of the criticism of "progressive education" in America. As was stated above, the expectation that students who have been conditioned to be dependent will suddenly rise to the demands of a democratic situation with skill and effective behavior is asking the impossible.

The bored student who, in a free situation, tells the teacher that he is bored may be using his freedom, but he is not using it skillfully. If he had developed skill, he would have taken into account *the needs of the receiver*—in this case the teacher—and the *clarity of the message* plus his own *personal responsibility* for the boring situation (why did he just sit around and let it get boring?). These three aspects of process skill may be looked at in detail as follows:

1. *Receiver needs.* Our receivers may very much need our messages. In this case the teacher needs to know that this student is bored if he is to deal with the problem. However, he also needs support and respect. Failing to receive these, he may block out or not hear the boredom message or he may feel hurt and counterattack the student, which will cause all sorts of bruised feelings *and not touch the boredom problem at all.* The student, then, has the alternative of (1) saying nothing verbally (*though the message will still come through non-verbally*), (2) saying, in a clumsy manner, that he is bored, or (3) communicating his problem to the teacher in a way that the teacher can accept without losing face and in a way that invites the teacher to help him, the student, to solve the problem.

2. *Clarity of message.* The need for training in process communication becomes evident whenever people attempt to tell others how they feel. The statement, "I am bored," is a case in point. Even if the teacher-receiver of this message is able to react to it unemotionally, what information does he have on which to base a helpful response? What

does boredom really mean? Does it mean that the student has other pressing problems on his mind, that he feels left out in the group, that he has finished the work and has nothing to do, that he does not know how to do the work and is frustrated, or does it mean something else? Until the teacher knows more than the bare word, boredom, he is not in any position to help.

3. *Personal responsibility.* Good teachers do not evade their responsibility for the success of the class—or, more precisely, for the success of each student within the class—but students evade this constantly. In fact, most students do not seem to recognize that there is any sphere of responsibility that *is* theirs This can be blamed on traditional teacher domination, but it seems sad and fruitless to dash about looking for someone to blame. As process skills are developed, the learning group and its teacher will begin to recognize a joint responsibility. And this, in turn, will help the two aspects detailed above under needs and clarity. If there is a joint responsibility, a student will be able to tell a teacher—or for that matter, a classmate—that he is bored without producing a defensive reaction on the part of the teacher. Rather than feeling offended or scapegoated, the teacher now will be free to react as he might to any request for help.

To test out the need for process skills, the reader should think of the most democratic classroom he has himself experienced and ask himself questions such as the following: "How free were the students to say what they really felt?" "How much personal responsibility did students feel for the success of the class?" "How much student-student interaction was there?" "To what degree was the teacher a member of the group?"

Effects of Blocked Process

In rare cases—particularly in some versions of the core curriculum—there has been and is a high degree of freedom and trust in classrooms. Most situations, however, cast the teacher in the role of benevolent despot doing things for students' own good whether they like it or not. With middle-class children who have been conditioned to this type approach there is not too much overt expression of frustration or aggressive behavior.

The little that does exist is taken care of by detentions, bad report cards, and expulsion. This is a suppression of feelings supported by school, teacher, and students plus the parents in most cases. Where the school attempts to deal with lower-class children, however, the teacher often finds himself alone in the support of suppression. These students are conditioned to express feelings more freely, but instead of dealing with them directly, the teacher is forced to fight against them. This is a difficult battle since these children are beyond the reach of the usual rewards and punishments. Thus, classroom dynamics are constantly at the boiling point, teachers are tense and irritable, and little learning occurs.

Unlike his more enculturated peers in the middle social classes, the lower-class youngster is forcing process awareness. He has not developed skill in doing this and therefore tends to offend and upset those around him, but he represents a fighting subculture that refuses to play the game of "Let's park our feelings outside and get down to cognitive endeavors as if we had no emotional responses." Most teachers have not developed methodology to respond to and clarify student reactions to themselves, to their teacher, to the school, and to life itself. Lacking such skills, teachers are forced into a bruising effort to force content learning on students who have not worked out a process readiness. In this situation, all they may be teaching is that the children are stupid and crude, that they really cannot succeed in academic work, and that the school is something to be feared, hated, and avoided at all costs. The result is tragic not only to the youngsters concerned but ultimately to the society in which they come to play a discordant role.

To this difficult situation, the school has most often responded by repeating the same old mistakes day after day. Many principals in depressed urban schools have advised their teachers: "Keep them busy and quiet. You can't really teach them anything because they do not appreciate education. But you can keep them from breaking the furniture and that is your job." Other more enlightened programs include special classes or special schools, which feature even tighter discipline, even heavier doses of academic trivia, and a great deal of industrial arts, home economics, and general vocational education. But the wood or metal shop has not proved to be the panacea for which educators prayed. The boy who does not succeed in the study of Shakespeare does not automatically respond to the making of a pump lamp. What he may need first and foremost is help in accepting himself and life as it exists, in seeing himself as a worthwhile person who *can* succeed in a number of areas, in seeing the effort to succeed as being worth the trouble, and in feeling that his peers and his teachers respect him as a human being. Lacking these simple but vital ingredients, he will continue in an active or a passive way to resist the most beautifully thought out curriculum revision, which provides only new buildings and shiny industrial shops. He needs these, but he also needs to talk *and be listened to.*

And his middle-class peers have the same needs! While they are more conforming and passive, they too are dropping out of school in increasing numbers. Unfortunately, they do not signal the alarm loudly by physically leaving the school. They are the psychological dropouts where the body comes day after day but the mind left last year.

The "teenie bopper" and "hippie" movements are crowded with children and older children of the middle class whose rallying cry is, "Don't trust anyone over thirty." They have developed peer support for their need to be respected as individuals and to be listened to when they speak. As larger and larger numbers drop out of school and out of society itself both physically and psychologically, the sermonizing, nagging voice of the classroom teacher who persists in teaching subject matter as if there were no emotions present becomes more and more ridiculous and, what is even more serious, less and less effective.

There is, then, a pressing need for process as well as content communication both for the general enhancement of learning and to cope with growing cultural pressure. In the mid-twentieth century, Americans find themselves at the threshold of a behavioral sciences explosion—a psychological renaissance. Its findings are sorely needed, and more practitioners, including classroom teachers, must be trained.

What has been dimly understood in the past concerning

human behavior and relationships will become more clear to future teachers (and to present teachers who keep abreast of modern developments in their field). The non-participating student, the underachiever, the "spoiled" child will be seen—are being seen—as people with needs that have not been met. Therapeutic techniques will not be as laden with taboo and fright (like those of witch doctors), and will be used with modifications to help the normal range of humans to develop as stronger, more self-directing personalities. Education of the present does a significant job of humanizing its students; education of the future will carry this process further by devoting specific attention to the effects of schooling and teachers upon the learner.

The Process Role of the Teacher

It is important for the classroom teacher who wishes to approach process communication in more than a hit or miss fashion to understand that he is *not* engaging in clinical psychology. Deep-seated emotional problems are not the business of the classroom. It is not within the scope of schooling objectives to probe people's psyches. This fact, however, should not serve the teacher as an excuse for dodging the problem of process awareness and process analysis in the classroom.

Careful examination of the procedures discussed in the previous chapters will show that the main effort is directed at freeing the expression of feelings that are already present and are probably being expressed unclearly and non-verbally. Such feelings (on the part of the teacher as well as student) not only affect what goes on in the class, but affect it in non-helpful ways. The emphasis of the present book is on bringing out and clarifying feelings, on building supporting norms for open, spontaneous behavior, and on developing verbal communication skills. In such classrooms, your best friend *will* tell you, and he will tell you in a clear, supportive, helpful way.

Teachers need not be psychologists, but they do need more education in the guidance area both in terms of skill and of the guidance point of view. The techniques detailed in the preceding chapters should provide a solid groundwork for further exploration of process communication *and* of its close interrelationship to content communication.

What is needed to bring teacher competency closer to the point where it can be considered truly professional is a revision of the traditionally muddled thinking concerning the teaching-learning operation. Process communication is not seen by a real professional as just one more nice little fad to be used when and if there is nothing else going on. Rather, it is seen as an integral part of content communication so that one cannot really be said to exist independent of the other. The whole child does indeed come into the classroom, *and the whole teacher comes in as well.*

Interaction Theory and Schooling

This interrelationship of communication levels set within a clearly thought-through theory of interaction is what the so-called guidance point of view has been struggling with throughout this century. What has been lacking is an integrated operational concept for the school, which would clearly delineate the duties, responsibilities, and spheres of influence of classroom teachers, guidance counselors, deans, and school psychologists.

The spelling out of these interlocking operations will be the task of a future book. Present purposes are served by the focus on the classroom social system. The best type of summary for this book would be a careful rereading followed by classroom tryouts of some of the procedures suggested. After doing this, the reader may compare his findings with the following in order to get a feeling of fitting the various pieces into an organic picture of schooling:

1. The American school and its society is undergoing physical and psychological change.
2. The physical change relates to population and knowledge explosions, which require accompanying changes in physical plant, staff, and curriculum organization.
3. The psychological change relates to increasing awareness of and demand for more openness in human communication.

4. Teaching and learning has been, historically, a teacher dominated one-way process composed of active teachers and passive learners. This posture on the part of the school will change more slowly than the expressed needs in the general culture, but it *will* change.
5. Agents of this change will be teachers and administrators working out of frameworks such as the one described in this book.
6. Teaching will be more tightly related to teaching theory as more knowledge becomes available concerning the behavioral outcomes of different teaching approaches.
7. Much of this knowledge will come from action research carried out at the classroom level by teachers who experiment with both process and content levels of communication in teaching.

Throughout this book the author has made a conscious effort to communicate with the reader on a direct and personal level. He has tried to anticipate process reactions of the reader and to discuss these thoroughly. On the content level, he has begun by attempting a rationale and conceptual framework underlying the interactive process of teaching and learning; has moved on to spell out, step by step, classroom tested procedures that may be used to cut through the communication barriers that have historically interfered with in-depth learning; has discussed and illustrated the problems of and procedures for gathering data concerning the success or failure of process activities, and has, finally, pulled at least some of the school and societal threads together to show the forces at work to move schooling from its traditional preoccupation with content communication toward a focus on *both content and process.*

What happens at this point is in the hands of the book's readers. Process analysis, with its opening up of human feelings, can be quite threatening, but it can also create a marvelous feeling of rapport and progress that lifts teaching to truly professional levels. It is time to stop cheating students (and teachers) out of a complete educational experience. If the contents of the present volume prove helpful to teachers who are looking for ways to increase the meaningfulness of student experience it will have fulfilled its purpose.

Bibliography

Albert, Harold B., *Reorganizing the High School Curriculum*. New York: Macmillan, 1962.

American Association of School Administrators, *Who's a Good Teacher?* Washington: AASA, Department of Classroom Teachers of the NEA, 1961.

Amidon, Edmund and Anita Simon, "Teacher-Pupil Interaction," *Review of Educational Research*, vol. 35, no. 2 (April, 1965).

——— and Ned A. Flanders, *The Role of the Teacher in the Classroom; a Manual for Understanding and Improving Teachers Classroom Behavior*. Minneapolis: Paul S. Amidon and Associates, 1963.

———, *The Role of the Teacher in the Classroom*. Minneapolis: Association for Productive Teaching, 1967.

Andrews, Kenneth R., ed., *The Case Method of Teaching Human Relations and Administration*. Cambridge: Harvard University Press, 1960.

Argyris, Chris, *An Introduction to Interaction Theory and Field Theory*. New Haven Labor and Management Center: Yale University, 1952.

Association for Supervision and Curriculum Development, *Perceiving, Behaving, Becoming*. Yearbook. Washington, D.C.: The Association, 1962.

Association for Supervision and Curriculum Development, NEA, *Theories of Instruction*. Washington, D.C.: The Association, 1965.

———, *The Way Teaching Is*. Washington, D.C.: The Association, 1966.

———, *Toward Better Teaching; A Report of Current Practices*. Washington, D.C.: Yearbook, 1949.

Bair, Medill and Richard G. Woodward, *Team Teaching in Action*. Boston: Houghton Mifflin Co., 1964.

Bellack, Arno A., et al., *The Language of the Classroom: Meanings Communicated in High School Teaching.* U.S. Dept. of Health, Education, and Welfare, Office of Education, Cooperative Research Project No. 1497. New York: Institute of Psychological Research, Columbia University, 1963.

————, *Theory and Research in Teaching.* New York: Bureau of Publications, Teachers College, Columbia University, 1963.

Benne, Kenneth D. and Paul Sheats, "Functional Roles of Group Members," *Journal of Social Issues.* 4, 2:41–49, 1948.

Berne, Eric L., *Games People Play; The Psychology of Human Relationships.* New York: Grove Press, 1964.

Biddle, Bruce J. and William J. Ellena, eds., *Contemporary Research on Teacher Effectiveness.* New York: Holt, Rinehart and Winston, 1964.

Bion, Wilfred R., *Experiences in Groups and Other Papers.* London: Tavistock Publications, 1961.

Bonner, Hubert, *Group Dynamics; Principles and Applications.* New York: Ronald Press, 1959.

Bowers, Norman D. and Robert S. Soar, *Studies of Human Relations in the Teaching-Learning Process.* V. Final Report: Evaluation of Laboratory Human Relations Training for Classroom Teachers. U.S. Department of Health, Education and Welfare, Office of Education. Cooperative Research Project n. 496. Chapel Hill, North Carolina: University of North Carolina, 1961.

Bradford, Leland, et al., *T-Group Theory.*

Brown, Bartley Frank, *The Non-Graded High School.* Englewood Cliffs, N.J.: Prentice-Hall, Inc., 1963.

Bullis, H. Edmund and Emily E. O'Malley, *Human Relations in the Classroom; Course I.* Wilmington, Delaware: The Delaware State Society for Mental Hygiene, 1954.

Cabot, Hugh and Joseph A. Kahl, *Human Relations; Concepts and Cases in Concrete Social Science.* Cambridge, Mass.: Harvard University Press, 1956.

Caldwell, Edson, *Group Techniques for the Classroom Teacher.* Chicago: Science Research Associates, 1960.

Cantor, Nathaniel, *The Dynamics of Learning,* 2nd Edition. Buffalo, New York: Foster and Steward, 1950.

Cartwright, Dorwin and Alvin Zander, eds., *Group Dynamics: Research and Theory,* 2nd Edition. Evanston, Illinois: Row, Peterson, 1960.

Coleman, J. S., *The Adolescent Society: The Social Life of the Teenager and Its Impact on Education.* New York: Free Press, 1961.

Collins, Barry E. and Harold Guetzkow, *A Social Psychology of Group Processes for Decision Making*. New York: Wiley, 1964.

Coleman, James C., *Personality Dynamics and Effective Behavior*. Fairlawn, N.J.: Scott, Foresman, 1960.

Cremin, Lawrence A., *The Transformation of the School*. New York: Knopf, 1961.

Deterline, William A., *Programed Instruction*. Englewood Cliffs, N.J.: Prentice-Hall, Inc., 1962.

Faunce, Roland C. and Morrel J. Clute, *Teaching and Learning in the Junior Highschool*. San Francisco: Wadsworth Publication Co., Inc., 1961.

Festinger, Leon, et al., *Theory and Experiment in Social Communication*. Ann Arbor: University of Michigan Press, 1950.

Flanders, Ned. A., *Teaching with Groups*. Minneapolis: Burgess Publishing Co., 1957.

Fox, Robert S., *Inventory of Teaching Innovations Directed Toward Improving Classroom Learning Atmospheres*. Ann Arbor, Michigan: Institute for Social Research, University of Michigan, 1961.

———— and Ronald Lippitt, "The Innovation of Classroom Mental Health Practices," Chapter 11 in Miles, Mathew B., *Innovation in Education*. New York: Bureau of Publications. Teachers College, Columbia University, 1964.

Gabriel, John, *An Analysis of the Emotional Problems of the Teacher in the Classroom*. Melbourne: F. W. Cheshire 1957.

Gage, Nathaniel L., Philip J. Runkel, and B. B. Chatterjee, *Equilibrium Theory and Behavior Change: An Experiment in Feedback From Pupils to Teachers*. Urbana: Bureau of Educational Research, College of Education, University of Illinois, 1960.

Garrett, Henry E., *The Art of Good Teaching*. New York: D. McKay Co., 1964.

Gibb, Jack R., Grace N. Platts, and Lorraine F. Miller, *Dynamics of Participative Groups*. Boulder, Colorado: University of Colorado, 1951.

———— and Lorraine M. Gibb, eds., "Spotlight on Members Roles," *Adult Leadership*, I, 8:2–23, January, 1953.

Golembiewski, Robert T., *The Small Group: An Analysis of Research Concepts and Operations*. Chicago: University of Chicago Press, 1962.

Goodlad, John I., and Robert H. Anderson, *The Non-Graded Elementary School*. New York: Harcourt, 1959.

Gordon, Thomas, *Group-Centered Leadership; A Way for Releasing the Creative Power of Groups.* Boston: Houghton-Mifflin Co., 1955.

Gorman, Alfred H., *The Leader in the Group.* New York: Bureau of Publications, Teachers College, Columbia University, 1963.

Gronlund, Norman E., *Sociometry in the Classroom.* New York: Harper, 1959.

Hare, A. Paul, *Handbook of Small Group Research.* New York: The Free Press, 1966.

———, Edgar F. Borgatta, and Robert F. Bales, eds., *Small Groups; Studies in Social Interaction.* New York: Alfred A. Knopf, 1955.

Harvey, O. J., *Motivation and Social Interaction; Cognitive Determinants.* New York: Ronald Press Co., 1963.

Hodgkinson, Harold L., *Educational Decisions: A Casebook.* Englewood Cliffs, N.J.: Prentice-Hall, Inc., 1963.

Hopkins, Thomas, *Interaction.*

Hughes, Marie, et al., *Development of the Means for Assessment of the Quality of Teaching in Elementary Schools.* Salt Lake City: University of Utah, 1959.

Hunter, Lottchen L., *Group Processes in Secondary School Mathematics.* Unpublished Doctoral Dissertation. Teachers College, Columbia University, 1951.

Huxley, Aldous, *Brave New World.* New York: Harper, 1946.

Jeep, H. A. and J. W. Hollis, "Group Dynamics in Action," *The Clearing House.* Vol. 41, No. 4, December, 1966.

Jourard, Sydney M., *The Transparent Self.* Princeton, N.J.: D. Van Nostrand, 1964.

Kaufman, Bel, *Up the Down Staircase.* Englewood Cliffs, N.J.: Prentice-Hall, Inc., 1964.

Kelley, Earl C., and Marie I. Rasey, *Education and the Nature of Man.* 1st Edition. New York: Harper, 1952.

———, *Education for What is Real.* New York: Harper, 1947.

Klein, Alan F., *Role Playing in Leadership Training and Group Problem Solving.* New York: Association Press, 1956.

Klein, Josephine, *Working With Groups; The Social Psychology of Discussion and Decision.* London: Hutchinson University Library, 1963.

Kohl, Herbert, *36 Children.* New York: The New American Library, 1967.

Kozol, Jonathan, *Death at an Early Age*. Boston: Houghton Mifflin, 1967.

Lewin, Kurt, *Field Theory in Social Science, Selected Theoretical Papers.* ed. by Dorwin Cartwright. 1st Edition. New York: Harper, 1951.

————, Ronald Lippitt, and Ralph K. White, "Patterns of Aggressive Behavior in Experimentally Created Social Climates," *Journal of Social Psychology.* X, 271–299, 1939.

Lewis, Sinclair, *Babbitt.* New York: Harcourt, 1950.

Lippitt, Ronald, and Elmer Van Egmond, eds., *Inventory of Classroom Study Tools for Understanding and Improving Classroom Learning Processes.* Ann Arbor, Michigan: Institute for Social Research, University of Michigan, 1962.

Lippitt, Ronald, and Ralph K. White, "The Social Climate of Children's Groups," in Roger Barker, Jacob Kounin, and Herbert Wright, *Child Development and Behavior.* New York: McGraw-Hill Book Co., 1943.

Llewellyn, Ardelle, and David Cahoon, "Teaching for Affective Learning," *Educational Leadership,* Vol. 22, no. 7, April, 1965.

Lott, Albert J., and Bernice E. Lott, *The Influence of Classroom Group Cohesiveness on Learning and Adherence to Standards.* Lexington, Kentucky: Research Foundation, University of Kentucky, 1964.

Lovegrove, John R., *A Collection of Practices on Small Group Learning for the Enrichment of the Secondary School Curriculum.* New York: Central School Boards Committee for Educational Research, 1955.

Lysaught, Jerome P., and Clarence Williams, *A Guide to Programmed Instruction.* New York: Wiley, 1963.

McGrath, Joseph E., and Irwin Altman, *Small Group Research.* New York: Holt, Rinehart, and Winston, Inc., 1966.

Maccoby, Eleanor E., Theodore Newcomb, and Eugene L. Hartley, *Readings in Social Psychology.* Third Edition. New York: Holt, 1958.

Mager, Robert F., *Preparing Objectives for Programmed Instruction.* San Francisco: Fearon Publishers, 1962.

Melby, Ernest O., *The Teacher and Learning.* Washington, D.C.: Center for Applied Research in Education, 1963.

Miles, Matthew B., *Learning to Work in Groups.* New York: Bureau of Publications, Teachers College, Columbia University, 1959.

Moreno, Jacob L., *Who Shall Survive?* New York: Beacon House, 1958.

Moustakes, Clark E., *The Alive and Growing Teacher.* New York: Philosophical Library, 1959.

———, *The Authenic Teacher; Sensitivity and Awareness in the Classroom.* Cambridge, Mass.: Howard A. Doyle Publishing Co., 1966.

———, *The Teacher and the Child; Personal Interaction in the Classroom.* New York: McGraw-Hill, 1956.

Murphy, Gardner, *Freeing Intelligence Through Teaching; A Dialectic of the Rational and the Personal.* New York: Harper, 1961.

Mursell, James L., *Successful Teaching; Its Psychological Principles.* 2nd Edition. New York: McGraw-Hill, 1954.

National Education Association, *Group Dynamics and Education.* Washington, D.C.: The Association, 1949.

National Society for the Study of Education, *The Dynamics of Instructional Groups: Sociopsychological Aspects of Teaching and Learning.* The 59th Yearbook, Part II, ed. by Nelson B. Henry, Chicago: The University of Chicago Press, 1960.

New York State University, Division of Research, *Group Dynamics and the Classroom Situation.* In Its Impact of Social and Economic Forces on Education, V. 3, 1953.

Olmsted, Michael S., *The Small Group.* New York: Random House, 1959.

Orwell, George, *1984.* New York: Harcourt, 1949.

Osborn, Alex F., *Applied Imagination: Principles and Procedures of Creative Problem-Solving.* New York: Charles Scribner's Sons, 1963.

Raths, Louis E., Merrill Harmin, and Sidney B. Simon, *Values and Teaching.* Columbus, Ohio: Charles E. Merrill Books, Inc., 1966.

Roethlisberger, F. J., and W. J. Dickson, *Management and the Worker.* Cambridge, Mass.: Harvard University Press, 1939.

Rogers, Carl R., *Client-Centered Therapy.* Boston: Houghton Mifflin, 1965.

Sarason, Seymour B., Kenneth Davidson, and Burton Blatt, *The Preparation of Teachers.* New York: John Wiley and Sons, Inc., 1962.

Sellitz, Claire, Marie Jahoda, Morton Deutch, and Stuart W. Cook, *Research Methods in Social Relations.* New York: Holt, 1959.

Shaplin, Judson T., and Henry F. Olds, Jr., eds., *Team Teaching.* New York: Harper, 1964.

Shipley, Charles M., et al., *A Synthesis of Teaching Methods*. New York: McGraw-Hill Co. of Canada, 1964.

Simpson, Ray H., *Improving Teaching-Learning Processes*. Longmans, Green and Co., New York: 1953.

Smith, B. Othanel, "A Concept of Teaching," *Teachers College Record*. Vol. 61:229–241 February, 1960.

—— and Milton O. Meux, *A Study of the Logic of Teaching*. Urbana: University of Illinois, 1963.

Smith, Louis M., *Group Process in Elementary and Secondary Schools*. Washington, D.C.: Department of Classroom Teachers, American Educational Research Association of the NEA, 1959.

Snygg, Donald, and Arthur W. Combs, *Individual Behavior: A Perceptual Approach to Behavior*. New York: Harper, 1959.

Sperle, D. Henryetta, *The Case Method Technique in Professional Training*. New York: Bureau of Publications, Teachers College, Columbia University, 1933.

Stogdill, Ralph M., *Individual Behavior and Group Achievement*. New York: Oxford University Press, 1959.

Taba, Hilda, *With Perspective on Human Relations; A Study of Peer Group Dynamics in an Eighth Grade*. Washington, D.C.: American Council on Education, 1955.

Thayer, V. T., *Passing of the Recitation*. Boston: D. C. Heath, 1928.

Thelen, Herbert A., *Dynamics of Groups at Work*. Chicago: University of Chicago Press, 1954.

——, "Experimental Research Toward a Theory of Instruction." *Journal of Educational Research*, 45, 89–136, 1951.

Thibault, John W., *The Social Psychology of Groups*. New York: Wiley, 1959.

Trump, J. Lloyd, and Dorsey Baynham, *Focus on Change*. Chicago: Rand McNally, 1961.

University of California at Los Angeles, Physical Education Department, *Group Processes in Physical Education*. ed. by Hilda C. Kozman. New York: Harper, 1951.

Watson, Goodwin, *Social Psychology: Issues and Insights*. Philadelphia: J. B. Lippincott, 1966.

Williams, Emlyn, *The Corn is Green*. New York: Random House, 1941.

Withall, J., "An Objective Measurement of a Teacher's Classroom Interaction," *Journal of Educational Psychology*. 47:203–12, 1956.

Zirbes, Laura, et al., "Fostering Individualization in the Classroom," pp. 75–97 of the *Yearbook of the Association for Supervision and Curriculum Development, 1964*.

——, *Spurs to Creative Teaching*. New York: Putnam, 1959.

Mike   Frankie

Keith   Dot